Annotated Legal Documents on Islam in Europe: Austria

Annotated Legal Documents on Islam in Europe

VOLUME 20

The titles published in this series are listed at *brill.com/ldie*

Annotated Legal Documents on Islam in Europe

Austria

Compiled, Annotated and Authored by

Richard Potz

BRILL

LEIDEN | BOSTON

Library of Congress Cataloging-in-Publication Data

Names: Potz, Richard, author.
Title: Annotated legal documents on Islam in Europe. Austria / compiled, annotated and authored by Richard Potz.
Description: Boston : Brill, 2021. | Series: Annotated legal documents on Islam in Europe, 2214-1340 ; 20 | Includes bibliographical references and index.
Identifiers: LCCN 2020046133 | ISBN 9789004445123 (paperback)
Subjects: LCSH: Muslims–Legal status, laws, etc.–Austria.
Classification: LCC KJJ2467.M56 P68 2021 | DDC 342.43608/5297–dc23
LC record available at https://lccn.loc.gov/2020046133

Typeface for the Latin, Greek, and Cyrillic scripts: "Brill". See and download: brill.com/brill-typeface.

ISSN 2214-1340
ISBN 978-90-04-44512-3 (paperback)

This book is printed on acid-free paper and produced in a sustainable manner.

Contents

Foreword by the Editors

This is the twentieth volume in the series *Annotated Legal Documents on Islam in Europe*. The publication of this series responds to the widespread lack of sound information about the legal status of Islam in Europe. In principle, this information is easily available to those who are willing to make the effort and know enough about the subject to ask the right questions of the digital search engines. But that requires both expertise and effort, and it takes place in an environment where the public political debate on Islam in many European countries is characterised by increasing concern and fear. Islam has come to be broadly perceived as a security issue rather than a religion like others in Europe. But the concern has also moved into the legal field, most markedly, of course, with discussions about limitations on Muslim female dress enacted in a growing number of countries, or the ban on building minarets on mosques in Switzerland, or restrictions on building mosques in certain Austrian provinces. At the same time, in a number of European states like Austria and Germany, legislation is enacted and state treaties are negotiated which aim to establish a stable and reliable basis for Muslim life and organisation. Even so, such measures are under scrutiny by an increasingly sceptical European public, sometimes ignoring the legal principles of secularity, not least the demands of state neutrality towards and equal treatment of all religions and beliefs regardless of numbers of adherents or public reputation.

In addition, the religious status and rights of Muslims in the various European countries differ significantly, due to different historical developments regarding the organisation of the relations between the state and religions. Furthermore, while in some states laws regulating such matters introduced decades ago are still in force and have to be re-interpreted in the face of a 'newcomer' religion, others have introduced new laws that consider the increasing religious plurality within Europe. Despite the common legal and political foundations constructed since 1945 in instruments such as the European Convention on Human Rights and the more recently accumulated legislation of the European Union, this closer look reveals remarkable differences due to the extent of separating state and religion or establishing co-operative structures. In some countries Islam has an officially recognised status which in some cases originated in the first half of the 20th century. In other countries no such recognition of any religion is available even if informal ways of favouring one religion over another may exist. Since 1990 especially, European courts have moved to equalise the status of Islam with that of other religions in the practical exercise of religious freedom in various countries. Particular practices regarded as core religious obligations—in the case of Muslims dress codes and practices such as male circumcision, access to correctly slaughtered meat and otherwise *halal* food, free time for the main periods of worship and religious festivals, and the right to build mosques—can be controversial in some countries while less so in others. In the course of the ongoing process of self-organisation and the participation of Muslims in civil societies and their co-operation with the state, children's access to Islamic religious instruction or the education of Muslim theologians can be achieved in co-operation with the state education systems in some countries, while in others the community must rely on its own arrangements. The practically pressing issue of financing the religious infrastructure is still far from being settled in many countries.

The aim of this series is to make this legislation available to both the interested researcher and the practising lawyer. Altogether the series is expected to comprise 32 volumes, one for each of the 27 countries of the European Union plus the United Kingdom, Norway and Switzerland, and a volume each dealing with the European Union (treaties, directives and decisions of the Court of Justice of the European Communities) and the European Court of Human Rights. Excerpts of relevant legislation are introduced and summarised by the volume compiler, and where court cases have provided significant interpretation of the law they will also be referred to. The legislation itself is reproduced in the original language, as the editors and the publisher agreed early on in the preparation of the series that any attempt to translate legislation into English would be unsatisfactory and risked being misleading. The comments and analysis by the author should give sufficient guidance to users to allow a decision as to whether to arrange a translation for their specific purposes.

Austria is a country of particular interest in the context of the present series. The Habsburg Empire, with Austria at its core, had a growing Muslim population as it progressively gained control of parts of the Ottoman Empire. While these Muslims usually maintained individual religious freedom, it was when Bosnia-Herzegovina was ceded by the Ottomans that a policy towards the Muslims of that province collectively had to be devised. This culminated in the recognition of Islam and its institutions in the Islam Act of 1912. The collapse of the now Austro-Hungarian Empire during the First World War meant that the Act soon became a dead letter. With the immigration of Muslims after the Second World War, especially but not only from Bosnia and Turkey, pressure rose to revive the Islam Act, a measure which was achieved in 1979. A new Act was passed in 2015, finally replacing the one of 1912.

An attempt has been made to ensure that the volumes are structured in as similar a manner as possible. The starting point for this has been the thematic organisation used variously in the *Yearbook of Muslims in Europe* which Brill has published annually since 2009. But it has been only a starting point, and in each volume the compiler and the editors have agreed on the structure which makes most sense for the legislation of the country concerned. Normally one member of the editorial group takes responsibility for discussing the structure and compilation of each volume with the compiler: in this instance, this task was undertaken by Prof. Jørgen Nielsen. We are also grateful to Kate Elliott for the care shown in copy editing the volume. The initiative for this project came from the publisher, where Nicolette van der Hoek and Nienke Brienen-Moolenaar have played an invaluable role in ensuring that the project has maintained its momentum. As editors, we appreciate how much their expertise contributes to ensuring that a project like this can run smoothly.

It is in the nature of such a project that each volume, if left as it stands, will gradually become out of date as new legislation and cases appear. From 2019 the series has become available online in a format which in due course will permit regular updating.

The Editors
July 2020

Preface

Starting from the protection of fundamental rights and based on the normative consideration of religious interests, religious law has increasingly become a cross-sectional matter touching practically all areas of law. In addition to the classic topics, such as the legal status envisaged for religious communities, marriage, financing systems and schools, new areas of law are being added, which sometimes almost become focal points of law on religion, such as integration law, anti-discrimination law and even security law. This development is mainly due to the pluralisation of society, caused not at least by migration.

In these contexts. the focus is usually put on Islam, which in Austria, as in almost all European countries, leads to the 'Islamisation' of the migration and integration debate. Dealing with Islam and Muslims thus becomes a touchstone and a challenge for the law on religion of the liberal democratic European states ruled by law. It is remarkable that such problems also exist in a country like Austria with experience of more than 100 years of integrating Islam into its system of legally recognised religious societies with public-law status.

Another Austrian feature is the controversial inclusion of those Alevi groups who emphasise their affiliation to Islam in the Austrian Islam Act 2015. Therefore, all Alevi groups were also included in this volume.

I have to thank in particular Brigitte Schinkele, whose critical reading accompanied the work on this book up to the final manuscript. Cornelia Tscheppe I have to thank for her help in preparing the manuscript.

Richard Potz

CHAPTER 1

Historical Background and Social Facts

1.1 Austria and Islam before the 19th Century

The first contacts with Islam happened for Austria in connection with the crusades. Austrian dukes and their knightly entourage participated in several crusades, which, in some cases, became part of the culture of remembrance. The second contact had a greater impact: from the 16th to the 18th century the long-drawn-out conflict with the Ottoman Empire was decisive for the Austrian state and the flourishing of the Habsburg monarchy in the 18th century. At this time the Austrian monarchy had emerged as a multiethnic collection of countries, put together in the defence against the Ottoman expansion. When, after a siege of eight weeks, the Ottomans were routed by a relieving army on 12 September 1683, the Habsburg monarchy counterattacked and, by expanding into Central and Southeastern Europe, became a European great power. This long-term military confrontation has also and above all been enshrined in Austrian memory as a Christian-Islamic conflict.

Since the Muslim inhabitants, unlike the Orthodox population, initially withdrew with the Ottoman army during the expansion of the Habsburgs in the Balkans, or emigrated to the Ottoman Empire after the conclusion of the peace treaties, the problem of Islamic minorities hardly arose at first.

In the peace of Passarowitz/Pozarevac in 1718, all Ottoman subjects were granted freedom of trade and the right to establish commercial offices and factories in the Habsburg territory. In addition, the domestic exercise of religion for Muslims of foreign citizenship was guaranteed.

According to a demographic census from January 1767, 134 Ottoman subjects were then living in Vienna with their families (13 Muslims, 82 Orthodox Christians, 21 Armenians and 18 Turkish Jews).

With the occupation of Bosnia and Herzegovina, the Habsburg Monarchy, entitled to administer the two provinces by Article XXV of the Berlin Treaty of 1878, for the first time faced the challenge of integrating an Islamic population in its territory. This also marked the beginning of a religious policy with an explicit focus on Islam that was originally determined by the specific conditions in Bosnia and Herzegovina.

After considerable difficulties at the beginning and the exodus of those Muslims who did not want to live under non-Muslim rule, the Austro-Hungarian administration was confronted with a rather conservative and backward part of the Ottoman Empire. Irrespective of the fact that it did not always act with providence and had to gather its experience and learn its lessons only painstakingly, cooperation with the dynamic forces in the country in the long term resulted in a remarkably European orientation of Bosnian Muslims which continues to determine their identity and self-perception to the present day.

The Austro-Hungarian Empire thus pursued a cautiously Islam-friendly line of policy which was most clearly reflected in the preparation and drafting of the Islam Act.[1] Throughout this process, the lessons learned and the experience the Bosnian administration had had with Islam and Muslims came to play a special role.

1.2 The Act on Islam 1912

The annexation of Bosnia in 1908 and the "definite and inseparable integration of Bosnia and Herzegovina" into the Habsburg monarchy (according to the report of the Special Commission on the drafting of the Act on Islam in 1910) resulted in the need to establish a legal status for Islam in Austria and Hungary which was equal to that of the traditional churches. Only a few weeks after the annexation of Bosnia and Herzegovina in 1908, representatives of Muslims living in Vienna sounded out whether there was "favourable disposition to granting Islam legal recognition" in the Austrian part of the monarchy. The competent ministry refused to deal with this submission for formal reasons, but, nevertheless, set up a working group to discuss the matter.

From the very beginning it was assumed that recognition according to the general provisions of the Recognition Act of 1874,[2] which were guided by Christian organisational structures, was not possible and therefore out of the question. In the course of the drafting process it was repeatedly mentioned that the main reason it was impossible to apply these regulations was that the formation of religious communities as stipulated in the Recognition Act was neither a given nor foreseeable. For the time being, the first goal was to ensure that adherents of Islam had the same legal status as members of the legally recognised churches and religious communities.

1 On the background and history of the Islam Act see Potz, Richard, "Das Islamgesetz 1912 und der religionsrechtliche Diskurs in Österreich zu Beginn des 20. Jahrhunderts", in Olechowski, Thomas, Neschwara, Christian, and Lengauer, Alina (eds), *Grundlagen der österreichischen Rechtskultur* (*FS Ogris 75*) (Vienna: Böhlau, 2010), pp. 385–408.

2 Cf. fn. 17.

This, however, brought up questions regarding the scope of this recognition. After an intensive discussion it was decided that only "Sunni Mohammedans of the Hanafite rite" should be included, because practically all Muslims in Bosnia and Herzegovina belonged to that school. It was argued that this would mean that under the law one [could] thus "easily favour the European-Mohammedan over his other fellow-believers [...]." This statement alludes to the traditional classification of the Hanafite school of religious law as "European-Islamic."[3]

In the case of marital law, which at that time was religiously oriented,[4] incorporation of the confessional marital law of Islam was considered hardly feasible. It was agreed that "marital law was the area in which one could make the smallest number of concessions to the Mohammedans." From the public administration point of view it was therefore necessary to insist on mandatory civil law marriage for Muslims.

In its statement of 1 April the Ministry of Justice insisted on the provision of broad protection under criminal law: "[a]ny religious practice that is recognised by the state shall be protected against gross disparagement as this hurts people's most holy and personal ideologies and feelings which could consequently trigger the most dangerous reaction and most seriously jeopardize public peace. Criticism and polemics voiced in an appropriate manner are not hindered or restricted by criminal law protection against mockery and humiliation."[5] The suggestion made by the Ministry of Justice was fully taken into account and Article 6 section 1 IslamG thus reads: "The religious community of the adherents of Islam according to the Hanafite rite shall, both as regards the community as such as well as religious worship and religious servants, enjoy the same legal protection as is granted to other legally recognised religious communities," and section 2 adds: "The doctrines of Islam, its institutions and customs shall enjoy the same protection, unless they are contrary to state law."[6]

The explanatory notes to the bill continue by stating that "it is without doubt that the scriptures on which the teachings of Islam are based, contain thoughts which, in many areas, cannot be denied grandness and depth, wisdom and poetry. [...] Considering these facts, one may in connection with the legislative

3 The discussions regarding the law's title were to regain topical importance many years later, when the addition "of Hanafite rite" was omitted following a decision by the Austrian Constitutional Court of 10 December 1987, VfSlg 11574/1987, cf. Chapter 1, fn. 12.

4 The Austrian Civil Law Code (ABGB) of 1812 contained different provisions for Catholics, other Christians and Jews according to their religious marriage law. This regulation was in force up to 1939.

5 Cf. Potz (fn. 1), 399.

6 Cf. the formulation of § 2 of the IslamG 2015, below chapter 3.

action requested indeed overlook some additional aspects that will not necessarily harmonise with the convictions of our moral cultural awareness."[7]

The bill passed through the parliamentary procedure in both chambers of Parliament (*Herrenhaus* and *Abgeordnetenhaus*), and the Act finally entered into force on 15 July 1912.[8] After the end of the Habsburg monarchy, the IslamG remained in force in the Austrian Republic,[9] without having any practical significance in the first half of the 20th century. In the second half of the century it became very helpful by creating specific conditions for the legal integration of Muslims in a Western and Central Europe state.

As far as Muslim life in the first republic is concerned, reference should be made in particular to the "Islamic Cultural League," a rather intellectual group founded in 1932 by Austrian Muslims. After the Second World War the *Moslemischer Sozialdienst* (Muslim Social Service) was established in 1962 on the initiative of Bosnian intellectuals. This not only provided social, religious and cultural services to Muslims in Austria but also strove to establish an Islamic community in Austria. The influx of Muslim students, refugees, diplomats and guest workers particularly in Vienna from the mid-1960s onwards also contributed to the increasing efforts towards having the recognition of 1912 eventually incorporated at institutional level, as is characteristic for Austrian religious legislation. On 26 January 1971, representatives of the *Moslemischer Sozialdienst* submitted a first application to this effect in Vienna. At first the question was raised whether an institutional establishment in accordance with the IslamG 1912 would be possible. Following lengthy negotiations with the governmental cultural authorities, a modified application was finally successful on 20 April 1979. In the preceding eight years of negotiations, some of the problems that had had to be faced in 1912 re-emerged—first and foremost the issue of the religious community's legal personality, internal rules, charter and organisation. On 2 May 1979 the establishment of the first religious community based on the Islam Act 1912 and the charter of the *Islamische Glaubensgemeinschaft in Österreich* (IGGÖ, Islamic Community in Austria) were positively acknowledged.[10]

7 Cf. Potz (fn. 1), 404.

8 RGBl. Nr. 159/1912.

9 In Czechoslovakia the Austrian Act on Islam remained in force before it was abrogated in October 1949 by Communist church-policy legislation. In 1916 a parallel law had been adopted for the Hungarian part of the Austro-Hungarian monarchy that also remained in force until the Communist takeover.

10 Cf. chapter 4.

The "expansion" to non-Hanafites was left to the Islamic community in agreement with the self-perception of Islam. According to the concept of the eight inter-Islamic accepted law schools (*madhāhib*),[11] legal recognition, therefore, was extended to the three other Sunni schools (Malikites, Shafiʾites and Hanbalites) and to the Twelver Shiites, Ibadites and Zaidites. Consequently, the Islamic Community referred to these seven schools of law in its charter.

In 1987, the Austrian Constitutional Court repealed the phrase "according to the Hanafite rite" in the Islam Act as unconstitutional.[12] In its reasoning the Constitutional Court stated that such a restriction represented a differentiation that was inadmissible for a religiously-neutral state and thus interfered with the Islamic Community's right to self-determination. The latter subsequently changed its charter. Since then "all adherents of Islam who have their residence in the Republic of Austria" have belonged to the IGGÖ (Article 1). This decision, however, meant that the issue of allocating those groups that actually referred to an Islamic tradition but had so far not been covered by the IGGÖ's constitution re-emerged as a pressing issue, especially in regard to the classification of the Alevis.[13]

Finally, the IslamG 1912 was renewed by the "Federal Act on the external legal relationships of Islamic Religious Societies" in 2015.[14]

1.3 Social Facts

In 2001 the last census in the traditional form of a questionnaire including a question on religious affiliation was held and 4.3% of Austrians declared themselves to be Muslims. From 2001 that type of census was replaced by register censuses, which are based on a combination of existing statistics and do not indicate the religious affiliation of the population. While the Catholic Church and Protestant Churches keep accurate statistics, taking withdrawals into account, with regard to other religious communities one has usually to rely on estimates. The most frequently mentioned figures for Islam and Alevites

11 In July 2005, a conference of Islamic scholars from 50 countries adopted the so-called Amman Declaration, which contains the recognition of eight law schools, adopted at the summit of the Organisation of the Islamic Conference in December 2005 and by the International Islamic Fiqh Academy in Jeddah. This recognition of the eight schools of law has a certain official character in the Muslim world.

12 VfGH 10. 12. 1987, VfSlg 11574/1987.

13 See chapter 5.

14 See chapter 3.

(7% and 1% respectively) are based not on self-declaration, but solely on national origin, and the assumption that the religious composition of immigrants is the same as that of people residing in their country of birth. This approach is known as the "random migrant assumption" and commonly used in migration studies. Due to questionable and inaccurate statistics in some countries—as for instance in the case of Turkey—they are, therefore, often hardly useful.

Initially Islam in Austria was shaped by citizens of Bosnian origin and their share increased after the first wave of labour migration from Yugoslavia in the 1960s and 1970s. Within a second wave of labour immigration in the 1970s and 1980s Turkish workers in particular came to Austria. Since the end of the 20th century Austria has been the destination for asylum seekers particularly from Bosnia, Syria, Afghanistan and Chechnya, which has led to a further pluralisation of Islam in Austria.

CHAPTER 2

The Status of Religious Communities in Austria

2.1 Fundamental Law Guarantees

Austrian constitutional law is exclusively written law, but it is not codified in a single document. After the fall of the Habsburg monarchy, the Federal Constitution of the Austrian Republic of 1920 brought about a significant constitutional change. Due to the failure to reach an agreement on a new catalogue of fundamental rights, the Constitutional Act on the Fundamental Rights of Citizens 1867 (StGG) was declared a constitutional law of the Federal State by Article 149 section 1 of the Federal Constitution 1920 (B-VG). Some Articles of the Treaty of St. Germain 1919 (StVStGermain) were adopted, too.[1] The European Convention on Human Rights (ECHR) has constitutional status in Austria, as well.

In these constitutional documents, freedom of religion is guaranteed in a comprehensive way, encompassing its individual, collective and corporate components. The enjoyment of political and civil rights is completely independent of any creed, religion or belief. Equal treatment and the prohibition of discrimination on religious grounds are guaranteed.

The most important provisions regarding the right to religious freedom are contained in the StGG of 1867. Guarantees of individual religious rights are embedded in Article 14 of the StGG and institutional guarantees in Article 15 of the StGG. Article 63 section 2 of the StVStGermain 1919 extended the right to free exercise of faith, religion or denomination of every kind in public as well as in private to every inhabitant in Austria, thus also to the adherents of non-recognised religious communities insofar as this exercise is not incompatible with public order or morality. The constitutional norm of Article 9 ECHR overlaps the older specific guarantees (freedom of belief, freedom of conscience, freedom of cult, freedom of confession) and summarises them in a way in one "aggregated law" on religious freedom in which the separate guarantees are combined. This comprehensive idea of religious freedom also makes it clear once and for all that not only is religious confession protected by constitutional order, but *Weltanschauung* (non-religious belief) is likewise protected.[2]

1 Chapter V, Part III (Protection of Minorities) of the Treaty of St. Germain, StGBl. Nr. 303/1920 as amended BGBl. II Nr. 154/1934.

2 See Schinkele, Brigitte, "Zur Weltanschauungsfreiheit in Österreich", in *Österreichisches Archiv für Kirchenrecht*, vol. 37 (1990), pp. 50–80.

There are also further guarantees in constitutional law aimed at protecting religious freedom; including especially general rules of non-discrimination relating, among other things, to differences in denomination. The general principle of equality is guaranteed in Article 2 of the StGG and in Article 7 of the B-VG. The right to religious freedom is furthermore functionally and systematically linked with other fundamental rights, such as freedom of expression, freedom of association and the right of assembly. Apart from guarantees related to religious freedom, only a few provisions explicitly refer to religion as such.[3]

There is no established church, and state and religious communities are institutionally separate. The diverse corporate activities of religious communities in the public sphere are guaranteed. The basic idea of this concept is to offer an adequate legal framework for the pluralistic inclusion of religious denominations into those public spheres in which the state does not exert its genuine sovereign power. The essential meaning of this concept is the consideration of the special features inherent to religious life and of cultural phenomena qualified as religious, restricted only by the well-known limitations of standards of human rights.

The neutrality of the state in matters of religion is a consequence of the guarantee of freedom of religion in connection with its commitment to non-discrimination on the basis of religion. As a result, the state is bound to denominational neutrality, which is described as a constitutional principle.[4] The fundamental principle of religious neutrality is carried out in practice in different ways. Consequently, one must make a clear distinction between two different forms of religious neutrality: "distancing" neutrality (*distanzierende Neutralität*) and "inclusive" neutrality (*hereinnehmende Neutralität*).[5] In as far as the state acts within its central sovereign sphere—i.e. where genuine non-exchangeable state tasks are concerned (for instance, jurisdiction)—religious neutrality must be realised in its "distancing" form, avoiding any reference to religious or philosophical beliefs.

A "religious neutral state" does not mean that the state is not allowed to set out measures of promotion in favour of religious communities as socially rel-

3 There is only one important area, namely the constitutional regulations regarding religion and school, cf. chapter 12.1.

4 Schlaich, Klaus, *Neutralität als verfassungsrechtliches Prinzip* (Tübingen: Mohr, 1972).

5 Böckenförde, Ernst-Wolfgang, "Kreuze (Kruzifixe) in Gerichtssälen? Zum Verhältnis von staatlicher Selbstdarstellung und religiös weltanschaulicher Neutralität des Staates", in *Zeitschrift für Evangelisches Kirchenrecht*, vol. 25 (1975), pp. 119–147; Kalb, Herbert, Potz, Richard, and Schinkele, Brigitte, *Das Kreuz in Klassenzimmer und Gerichtssaal* (Freistadt: Plöchl, 1996), pp. 36–55.

evant factors. Thus, the denominational neutrality of the state must be carried out in a cooperative way that integrates aspects of religion and belief, and, of course, without discrimination or identification with any particular denomination on the part of the state.

The successive recognition of religious communities since 1867 in a process of emancipation has incorporated more and more religious communities into a system of legal recognition on the same level as the historically dominant Catholic Church. Corporate guarantees for these religious communities constitute a basis for a characteristic institutionalism in Austrian law on religion. There is a system of different—nowadays three—options for the legal status of religious communities:

- Legally recognised churches and religious societies with public-law status[6]
- State-registered religious communities with legal personality under private law in accordance with a special Law on Religious Associations[7]
- Religious communities with legal personality under private law based on the general Law on Associations.

Staatsgrundgesetz vom 21. Dezember 1867 über die allgemeinen Rechte der Staatsbürger (Staatsgrundgesetz—StGG 1867)
RGBl. Nr. 142/1867[8] as amended BGBl. Nr. 684/1988

…

Art. 14

(1) Die volle Glaubens- und Gewissensfreiheit ist Jedermann gewährleistet.
(2) Der Genuß der bürgerlichen und politischen Rechte ist von dem Religionsbekenntnisse unabhängig; doch darf den staatsbürgerlichen Pflichten durch das Religionsbekenntniß kein Abbruch geschehen.

6 The following churches and religious societies enjoy public law status: the Catholic Church, the Protestant Church, Greek-Oriental Churches, Oriental-Orthodox Churches (the Armenian-Orthodox Church, the Syrian-Orthodox Church, the Coptic-Orthodox Church), the Hebrew Religious Community, the Islamic Religious Community, the Old Catholic Church, the Evangelical-Methodist Church, the Church of Jesus Christ of the Latter-day Saints (Mormons), the New Apostolic Church, the Buddhist Religious Community, Jehova's Witnesses, the Alevi Islamic Religious Community and the Free Churches in Austria.

7 See chapter 2.3.

8 The Constitutional Act on the Fundamental Rights of Citizens 1867 (StGG), RGBl. Nr. 142/1867, was declared a constitutional law of the Federal State by Article 149 section 1 of the Federal Constitution 1920 (B-VG), BGBl. Nr. 1/1920.

(3) Niemand kann zu einer kirchlichen Handlung oder zur Theilnahme an einer kirchlichen Feierlichkeit gezwungen werden, in sofern er nicht der nach dem Gesetze hiezu berechtigten Gewalt eines Anderen untersteht.

Art. 15

Jede gesetzlich anerkannte Kirche und Religionsgesellschaft hat das Recht der gemeinsamen öffentlichen Religionsübung, ordnet und verwaltet ihre inneren Angelegenheiten selbständig, bleibt im Besitze und Genusse ihrer für Cultus-, Unterrichts- und Wohlthätigkeitszwecke bestimmten Anstalten, Stiftungen und Fonde, ist aber, wie jede Gesellschaft, den allgemeinen Staatsgesetzen unterworfen.

Art. 17

(1) Die Wissenschaft und ihre Lehre ist frei.
(2) Unterrichts- und Erziehungsanstalten zu gründen und an solchen Unterricht zu ertheilen, ist jeder Staatsbürger berechtigt, der seine Befähigung hiezu in gesetzlicher Weise nachgewiesen hat.[9]
(3) Der häusliche Unterricht unterliegt keiner solchen Beschränkung.[10]
(4) Für den Religionsunterricht in den Schulen ist von der betreffenden Kirche oder Religionsgesellschaft Sorge zu tragen.[11]
(5) Dem Staate steht rücksichtlich des gesammten Unterrichts- und Erziehungswesens das Recht der obersten Leitung und Aufsicht zu.
Staatsvertrag von Saint-Germain-en Laye vom 10. September 1919 (StVSt-Germain)
StGBl. Nr. 303/1920[12] as amended BGBl. II Nr. 154/1934
Art. 63

(1) Österreich verpflichtet sich, allen Einwohnern Österreichs ohne Unterschied der Geburt, Staatsangehörigkeit, Sprache, Rasse oder Religion vollen und ganzen Schutz von Leben und Freiheit zu gewähren.

9 See chapter 12.6.
10 There is no explicit regulation regarding religious motivation for home-schooling.
11 See chapter 12.5.
12 These Articles of the Treaty of St. Germain 1919, BGBl. Nr. 303/1920, were declared a constitutional law of the Federal State by Article 149 section 1 of the Federal Constitution (B-VG) 1920.

(2) Alle Einwohner Österreichs haben das Recht, öffentlich oder privat jede Art Glauben, Religion oder Bekenntnis frei zu üben, sofern deren Übung nicht mit der öffentlichen Ordnung oder mit den guten Sitten unvereinbar ist.

…

Art. 67

Österreichische Staatsangehörige, die einer Minderheit nach Rasse, Religion oder Sprache angehören, genießen dieselbe Behandlung und dieselben Garantien, rechtlich und faktisch, wie die anderen österreichischen Staatsangehörigen; insbesondere haben sie dasselbe Recht, auf ihre eigenen Kosten Wohlthätigkeits-, religiöse oder soziale Einrichtungen, Schulen und andere Erziehungsanstalten zu errichten, zu verwalten und zu beaufsichtigen mit der Berechtigung, in denselben ihre eigene Sprache nach Belieben zu gebrauchen und ihre Religion frei zu üben.

Europäische Konvention zum Schutze der Menschenrechte und Grundfreiheiten vom 4. November 1950 (EMRK)
BGBl. Nr. 210/1958[13] as amended BGBl. III Nr. 139/2018

Art. 9—*Gedanken-, Gewissens- und Religionsfreiheit*

(1) Jedermann hat Anspruch auf Gedanken-, Gewissens- und Religionsfreiheit; dieses Recht umfaßt die Freiheit des einzelnen zum Wechsel der Religion oder der Weltanschauung sowie die Freiheit, seine Religion oder Weltanschauung einzeln oder in Gemeinschaft mit anderen öffentlich oder privat, durch Gottesdienst, Unterricht, Andachten und Beachtung religiöser Gebrauche auszuüben.
(2) Die Religions- und Bekenntnisfreiheit darf nicht Gegenstand anderer als vom Gesetz vorgesehener Beschränkungen sein, die in einer demokratischen Gesellschaft notwendige Maßnahmen im Interesse der öffentlichen Sicherheit, der öffentlichen Ordnung, Gesundheit und Moral oder für den Schutz der Rechte und Freiheiten anderer sind.

13 According to Article II no. 7 Bundesverfassungsgesetz BGBl. Nr. 59/1964, the ECHR is elevated to constitutional status.

(1.) Zusatzprotokoll zur EMRK vom 20. März 1952
BGBl Nr. 210/1958[14]

Art. 2—*Recht auf Bildung*

Das Recht auf Bildung darf niemandem verwehrt werden. Der Staat hat bei Ausübung der von ihm auf dem Gebiet der Erziehung und des Unterrichts übernommenen Aufgaben das Recht der Eltern zu achten, die Erziehung und den Unterricht entsprechend ihren eigenen religiösen und weltanschaulichen Überzeugungen sicherzustellen.

2.2 Legally Recognised Churches and Religious Societies

2.2.1 *The Historical Background*

The constitutional basis of legally recognised churches and religious societies is laid down in Article 15 of the StGG.[15] The right of self-determination as it is encompassed there implies the status of an incorporated body under public law (corporations *sui generis*).

Article 15 of the StGG does not contain any details concerning either the preconditions for recognition of religious communities or the rules of the procedure to be followed. Therefore, the Act on Legal Recognition of Religious Communities was enacted in 1874 (*Anerkennnungsgesetz*, AnerkG[16]) and is still in force.[17] According to § 1 of the Act adherents of a hitherto not legally recognised faith are granted recognition as a religious community provided that the following conditions are met: firstly, that their religious doctrine, forms of worship, constitution and chosen name contain nothing illegal or immoral; and, secondly, that the establishment and continued existence of a religious community, fulfilling at least the requirements of this law, are ensured.

The legal positions and the external legal relationships concerning "historically recognised" churches and religious societies have been defined by means of

14 According to Article II no. 7 Bundesverfassungsgesetz BGBl. Nr. 59/1964, the Additional Protocol 1 ECHR is elevated to constitutional status.

15 See chapter 2.1.

16 RGBl. Nr. 68/1874.

17 This law is not printed here, though it could be of importance for the Alevite Federation, which has denied the applicability first of the IslamG 1912 and now of the IslamG 2015 for itself, cf. chapter 1.1.

special laws (Concordat 1933/34,[18] ProtestantenG 1961,[19] OrthodoxenG 1967,[20] IsraelitenG 1890 as amended in 2012[21]). Islam also belongs to this group because of the inapplicability of the Recognition Act 1874 (IslamG 1912).[22] The amendment by the IslamG 2015 contains a further particularity because it regulates not only the legal status of the existing Islamic or (Islamic) Alevi Religious Society[23] but also includes special provisions for the legal recognition of other Islamic religious societies.[24]

The specific legislation is usually legitimised by achieving material equality in a better way, considering the specificities of individual religious societies. Although they have essentially similar content, they do address the differences between communities.

2.2.2 *Public Law Status*

Legal recognition as presupposed in Article 15 of the StGG implies the status of an incorporated body under public law (corporations *sui generis*) which is explicitly laid down in the special laws for individual churches and religious societies, as, for example, in § 1 of the IslamG 2015. Nevertheless, legally recognised churches and religious societies do not have the essential characteristics of public law corporations in the sense of administrative law. They are neither state-established institutions nor have they been given sovereign power. By their very nature they lie outside state structures, and their legislative, administrative and judicial acts are not subject to state surveillance. They are generally included whenever state legislation relates to corporations under public law, unless explicitly excluded by law, as is the case, for instance, in the Act on Audiovisual Media Services.[25]

18 BGBl. II Nr. 2/1934.

19 Bundesgesetz über äußere Rechtsverhältnisse der Evangelischen Kirche, BGBl. Nr. 183/1961 as amended BGBl. I Nr. 92/2009.

20 Bundesgesetz über äußere Rechtsverhältnisse der griechisch-orientalischen Kirche in Österreich, BGBl. Nr. 229/1967 as amended BGBl. I Nr. 68/2011.

21 Gesetz betreffend die Regelung der äußeren Rechtsverhältnisse der israelitischen Religionsgesellschaft, RGBl. Nr. 57/1890 as amended BGBl. I Nr. 48/2012.

22 Cf. chapter 1.1.

23 See chapters 3 and 5.

24 See chapter 3.

25 Cf. § 10 section 2 Bundesgesetz über audiovisuelle Mediendienste, BGBl. I Nr. 84/2001 as amended BGBl. I Nr. 86/2015, according to which legally recognised churches and religious societies are to be accepted as private providers of media services, regardless of their public-law status, because they do not fulfil state functions characteristic of public-law corporations.

The legislator of the StGG 1867 considered public-law status as an instrument for exercising state influence on churches and religious societies. Since then, the relationship between state and church, as well as constitutional reality and the methods of constructing fundamental rights, has changed significantly. Based on the separation of state and church at the institutional level, being granted this status nowadays implies an offer to cooperate with the state in certain aspects. The so-called "legitimate constitutional expectations" from the religious communities primarily concern their contributions in the sphere of education, social and welfare activities, as well as their role as dialogue partners regarding the complex ethical issues the modern state must deal with. This status makes clear that the state accepts the activity of churches and religious societies in the public area and does not wish to displace them into the private sphere. In many legal fields significant consequences are derived from public-law status.[26]

2.3 State-Registered Religious Denominational Communities

The Act on the Legal Personality of Religious Denominational Communities (*Bundesgesetz über die Rechtspersönlichkeit von religiösen Bekenntnisgemeinschaften*, BekGG)[27] of 1998 created the legal basis for religious communities to obtain legal personality without at the same time giving them the status of a public-law corporation. Registered religious denominational communities acquire juridical personality under private law and therefore do not enjoy the "privileges" granted by law to legally recognised churches and religious societies. The differentiation between legally recognised and non-recognised religious communities is constitutionally laid down in Article 15 of the StGG.[28] As a result, legal consequences of public-law status are provided for by ordinary law in numerous areas. The most important fields of law containing different regulations for both categories of religious communities are the right of self-determination, the subsidising of private denominational schools, religious instruction classes, revenue law, labour law, military and non-military service and exemptions concerning the employment of foreigners. These differences in treatment within various legal spheres have remarkable consequences for the religious community concerned as well as its individual adherents.

26 See chapter 2.3.1.

27 BGBl. I Nr. 19/1998 as amended BGBl. I Nr. 75/2013.

28 See chapter 2.1.

Evidence must be submitted with the application that the religious community has at least 300 followers residing in Austria who do not belong to any other religious denominational community with legal personality, legally recognised church or religious community (§ 3 section 3). According to § 4 section 1 no. 2 the religious doctrine of the community must be set out, which must differ from the doctrine of already existing religious confessional communities according to this federal law as well as from that of legally recognised churches and religious societies.

The administrative body is obliged to refuse the acquisition of legal personality if this is necessary with regard to the doctrine or its practice for the protection of the interests of public safety, public order, health and morals or the protection of the rights and freedoms of others in a democratic society. This is especially the case regarding incitement to commit an illegal punishable action, hindering the psychological development of young adults, and causing damage to psychological integrity by the use of psychotherapeutic methods especially aimed at winning converts (§ 5).

Of the Islamic tradition, the Baha'is obtained registration as a religious confessional community on 11 July 1998. After a decision of the Constitutional Court[29] the "Islamic Alevite confessional community in Austria" (IAGÖ) acquired legal personality as a religious confessional community with effect from 13 December 2010.[30] The application of the "Federation of Alevi Communities in Austria" (AABF) for registration as "Alevi Religious Society in Austria," however, was rejected on 17 December 2010.[31] The *Islamisch-Schiitische Glaubensgemeinschaft in Österreich* (*Schia*) ("Islamic-Shiite Religious Community in Austria/Shia") was registered on 1 March 2013.[32] The *Alt-Alevitische Glaubensgemeinschaft in Österreich* ("Old Alevi Religious Community") acquired legal personality with effect from 23 August 2013.[33]

Bundesgesetz über die Rechtspersönlichkeit von religiösen Bekenntnisgemeinschaften (Bekenntnisgemeinschaftengesetz—BekGG)
BGBl. I Nr. 19/1998 as amended BGBl. I Nr. 75/2013

29 Cf. chapter 5.

30 Meanwhile the IAGÖ was recognised and integrated in the IslamG 2015, BGBl. I Nr. 39/2015, (cf. chapter 3 and 5).

31 See chapter 5.

32 See chapter 6.2.

33 See chapter 7.2.

§ 1—*Begriff der religiösen Bekenntnisgemeinschaft*

Religiöse Bekenntnisgemeinschaften im Sinne dieses Bundesgesetzes sind Vereinigungen von Anhängern einer Religion, die gesetzlich nicht anerkannt sind.

§ 2—*Erwerb der Rechtspersönlichkeit für eine religiöse Bekenntnisgemeinschaft*

(1) Religiöse Bekenntnisgemeinschaften erwerben die Rechtspersönlichkeit nach diesem Bundesgesetz durch Antrag beim Bundesminister für Unterricht und kulturelle Angelegenheiten nach Ablauf einer Frist von sechs Monaten nach dem Einlangen dieses Antrages, wenn nicht innerhalb dieser Frist ein Bescheid über die Versagung der Rechtspersönlichkeit (§ 5) zugestellt worden ist.
(2) Der Bundesminister für Unterricht und kulturelle Angelegenheiten hat das Einlangen von Anträgen gemäß Abs. 1 im „Amtsblatt zur Wiener Zeitung" kundzumachen.
(3) Über den Erwerb der Rechtspersönlichkeit ist ein Feststellungsbescheid zu erlassen, der den Namen der religiösen Bekenntnisgemeinschaft sowie die nach außen vertretungsbefugten Organe in allgemeiner Bezeichnung zu enthalten hat.
(4) Mit dem Feststellungsbescheid nach Abs. 3 hat der Bundesminister für Unterricht und kulturelle Angelegenheiten die Auflösung jener Vereine zu verbinden, deren Zweck in der Verbreitung der Religionslehre der betreffenden religiösen Bekenntnisgemeinschaft besteht.
(5) Wird eine religiöse Bekenntnisgemeinschaft unter Auflösung eines Vereines, der der Unterstützung des betreffenden religiösen Bekenntnisses dient, neu gebildet, so ist abgabenrechtlich von einem bloßen Wechsel der Rechtsform und weiterem Fortbestehen ein und desselben Steuerpflichtigen (Rechtsträgers) auszugehen.
(6) Religiöse Bekenntnisgemeinschaften mit Rechtspersönlichkeit nach diesem Bundesgesetz haben das Recht, sich als „staatlich eingetragene religiöse Bekenntnisgemeinschaft" zu bezeichnen.

§ 3—*Antrag der religiösen Bekenntnisgemeinschaft auf Erwerb der Rechtspersönlichkeit*

(1) Der Antrag der religiösen Bekenntnisgemeinschaft auf Erwerb der Rechtspersönlichkeit hat durch die Vertretung der religiösen Bekenntnt-

nisgemeinschaft zu erfolgen. Die Vertretungsbefugnis ist glaubhaft zu machen. Ferner ist eine Zustelladresse anzugeben.
(2) Dem Antrag sind Statuten und ergänzende Unterlagen beizulegen, aus denen sich Inhalt und Praxis des Religionsbekenntnisses ergeben.
(3) Zusammen mit dem Antrag ist der Nachweis zu erbringen, daß der religiösen Bekenntnisgemeinschaft mindestens 300 Personen mit Wohnsitz in Österreich angehören, welche weder einer religiösen Bekenntnisgemeinschaft mit Rechtspersönlichkeit nach diesem Bundesgesetz noch einer gesetzlich anerkannten Kirche oder Religionsgesellschaft angehören.
(4) Im Bundesgebiet bestehende Vereine, deren Zweck in der Verbreitung der Religionslehre der religiösen Bekenntnisgemeinschaft besteht, haben im Verfahren Parteistellung; sie sind mit dem Antrag namhaft zu machen.

§ 4—*Statuten*

(1) Die Statuten haben zu enthalten:
1. Name der religiösen Bekenntnisgemeinschaft, welcher so beschaffen sein muß, daß er mit der Lehre der religiösen Bekenntnisgemeinschaft in Zusammenhang gebracht werden kann und Verwechslungen mit bestehenden religiösen Bekenntnisgemeinschaften mit Rechtspersönlichkeit und gesetzlich anerkannten Kirchen und Religionsgesellschaften oder deren Einrichtungen ausschließt,
2. Darstellungen der Religionslehre, welche sich von der Lehre bestehender religiöser Bekenntnisgemeinschaften nach diesem Bundesgesetz sowie von der Lehre gesetzlich anerkannter Kirchen und Religionsgesellschaften unterscheiden muß,
3. Darstellungen der sich aus der Religionslehre ergebenden Zwecke und Ziele der religiösen Bekenntnisgemeinschaft sowie Rechte und Pflichten der Angehörigen der religiösen Bekenntnisgemeinschaft,
4. Bestimmungen betreffend den Beginn der Mitgliedschaft und die Beendigung der Mitgliedschaft, wobei die Beendigung jedenfalls gemäß § 8 Abs. 1 gewährleistet sein muß,
5. Art der Bestellung der Organe der religiösen Bekenntnisgemeinschaft, deren sachlicher und örtlicher Wirkungskreis, Sitz und Verantwortlichkeit für den staatlichen Bereich,
6. Vertretung der religiösen Bekenntnisgemeinschaft nach außen,
7. Art der Aufbringung der für die Erfüllung der wirtschaftlichen Bedürfnisse erforderlichen Mittel,

8. Bestimmungen für den Fall der Beendigung der Rechtspersönlichkeit, wobei insbesondere sicherzustellen ist, daß Forderungen gegen die religiöse Bekenntnisgemeinschaft ordnungsgemäß abgewickelt werden und das Vermögen der religiösen Bekenntnisgemeinschaft nicht für Zwecke verwendet wird, die ihrer Zielsetzung widersprechen.
(2) In den Statuten kann vorgesehen werden, daß auch örtliche Teilbereiche der religiösen Bekenntnisgemeinschaft eigene Rechtspersönlichkeit erwerben können. In diesem Fall haben die Statuten bezüglich der Teilbereiche zu bestimmen:
1. Bezeichnung des örtlichen Wirkungsbereiches,
2. eigene vertretungsberechtigte Organe,
3. Bestimmungen betreffend den Rechtsübergang bei Auflösung dieses Rechtsträgers.

§ 5—*Versagung des Erwerbs der Rechtspersönlichkeit*

(1) Der Bundesminister für Unterricht und kulturelle Angelegenheiten hat den Erwerb der Rechtspersönlichkeit zu versagen, wenn
1. dies im Hinblick auf die Lehre oder deren Anwendung zum Schutz der in einer demokratischen Gesellschaft gegebenen Interessen der öffentlichen Sicherheit, der öffentlichen Ordnung, Gesundheit und Moral oder zum Schutz der Rechte und Freiheiten anderer notwendig ist; dies ist insbesondere bei Aufforderung zu einem mit Strafe bedrohtem gesetzwidrigen Verhalten, bei einer Behinderung der psychischen Entwicklung von Heranwachsenden, bei Verletzung der psychischen Integrität und bei Anwendung psychotherapeutischer Methoden, insbesondere zum Zwecke der Glaubensvermittlung, gegeben,
2. die Statuten dem § 4 nicht entsprechen.
(2) Die Versagung der Rechtspersönlichkeit ist im „Amtsblatt zur Wiener Zeitung“ kundzumachen.

§ 6—*Erwerb der Rechtspersönlichkeit für örtliche Teilbereiche einer religiösen Bekenntnisgemeinschaft*

Der Erwerb der Rechtspersönlichkeit für örtliche Teilbereiche einer religiösen Bekenntnisgemeinschaft bedarf eines Antrages durch die religiöse Bekenntnisgemeinschaft beim Bundesminister für Unterricht und kulturelle Angelegenheiten und wird mit dem Tag des Einlangens wirksam. Der Bundesminister für Unterricht und kulturelle Angelegenheiten hat das Einlangen des Antrages zu bestätigen.

§ 7—*Mitteilungspflichten der religiösen Bekenntnisgemeinschaft mit Rechtspersönlichkeit*

Religiöse Bekenntnisgemeinschaften und deren Teilbereiche mit Rechtspersönlichkeit haben die Namen und Anschriften ihrer jeweiligen vertretungsberechtigten Organe sowie jede Änderung der Statuten unverzüglich dem Bundesministerium für Unterricht und kulturelle Angelegenheiten bekanntzugeben. Die Kenntnisnahme ist bescheidmäßig zu versagen, wenn eine statutenwidrige Bestellung der Organe der Behörde zur Kenntnis gelangt ist bzw. die Statutenänderung den Grund für eine Versagung gemäß § 5 geben würde.

§ 8—*Beendigung der Mitgliedschaft zu einer religiösen Bekenntnisgemeinschaft*

(1) Die Beendigung der Mitgliedschaft zu einer religiösen Bekenntnisgemeinschaft erfolgt jedenfalls durch die Erklärung des Austrittes vor der Bezirksverwaltungsbehörde. Diese hat den Austritt der betreffenden religiösen Bekenntnisgemeinschaft mitzuteilen.
(2) Gebühren anläßlich des Austrittes dürfen nicht gefordert werden.

§ 9—*Beendigung der Rechtspersönlichkeit*

(1) Die Rechtspersönlichkeit endet durch
1. Selbstauflösung, die dem Bundesminister für Unterricht und kulturelle Angelegenheiten schriftlich bekanntzugeben ist,
2. Aberkennung der Rechtspersönlichkeit.
(2) Der Bundesminister für Unterricht und kulturelle Angelegenheiten hat einer religiösen Bekenntnisgemeinschaft oder deren Teilbereich die Rechtspersönlichkeit abzuerkennen, wenn
1. sie eine der für den Erwerb der Rechtspersönlichkeit maßgeblichen Voraussetzungen nicht oder nicht mehr erbringt,
2. sie durch mindestens ein Jahr keine handlungsfähigen vertretungsbefugten Organe für den staatlichen Bereich besitzt,
3. bei Vorliegen der Voraussetzungen für eine Versagung der Rechtspersönlichkeit gemäß § 5, sofern trotz Aufforderung zur Abstellung des Aberkennungsgrundes dieser fortbesteht, oder
4. bei statutenwidrigem Verhalten, sofern trotz Aufforderung zur Abstellung dieses fortbesteht.

(3) Die Aberkennung der Rechtspersönlichkeit ist im „Amtsblatt zur Wiener Zeitung" kundzumachen.

§ 10—*Register über die religiösen Bekenntnisgemeinschaften mit Rechtspersönlichkeit*

(1) Der Bundesminister für Unterricht und kulturelle Angelegenheiten hat ein Register über die religiösen Bekenntnisgemeinschaften mit Rechtspersönlichkeit zu führen. Dieses hat zu enthalten:
1. Name der religiösen Bekenntnisgemeinschaft,
2. Rechtspersönlichkeiten für Teilbereiche,
3. Geschäftszahl und Datum des Feststellungsbescheides gem. § 2 Abs. 3,
4. vertretungsbefugte Organe und Zeichnungsberechtigung,
5. bei Beendigung der Rechtspersönlichkeit den Grund.
(2) Das Register ist öffentlich.
(3) Auf Verlangen ist jedermann Auskunft über die Anschrift der religiösen Bekenntnisgemeinschaft und über deren nach außen vertretungsbefugten Mitglieder zu erteilen. Ferner ist auf Antrag der religiösen Bekenntnisgemeinschaft oder auch sonst von Personen oder Institutionen, die ein berechtigtes Interesse glaubhaft machen, eine Bestätigung darüber auszustellen, wer nach den vorliegenden Statuten sowie nach den Meldungen gemäß § 7 zur Vertretung nach außen befugt ist.

§ 11[34]—*Zusätzliche Voraussetzungen für eine Anerkennung nach dem Anerkennungsgesetz*

Schlußbestimmungen

§ 12

Dieses Bundesgesetz tritt mit dem auf die Kundmachung folgenden Tag in Kraft.

§ 13.

Mit der Vollziehung des § 2 Abs. 5 ist der Bundesminister für Finanzen, im übrigen der Bundesminister für Unterricht und kulturelle Angelegenheiten betraut.

---

34 This paragraph contains an amendment to the AnerkG 1874: see fn. 17.

2.4 Religious Communities as Non-profit Associations

According to § 1 section 1 of the Act on Associations 2002 (*Bundesgesetz über Vereine*, VereinsG)[35] non-profit (ideological) associations are voluntary organisations consisting of at least two persons set up for a long period of time on the basis of statutes pursuing certain non-profit purposes. This law does not apply to those associations which have to be constituted with a different legal status according to other legal provisions or which have freely chosen another legal form under the appropriate legislation (§ 1 section 2). Henceforth, it is clear that religious communities can also obtain legal personality under private law on the basis of the VereinsG 2002.[36] With respect to the previous Act on Associations, such an option has been denied for a long time, and later the respective regulation has been understood to be controversial, which resulted in an uncertain legal situation. Religious communities will refer to this possibility if they do not fulfil the conditions for legal recognition or state-registration, or if legal entity under public law is not in concordance with their self-understanding. These organisations enjoy equal status with other private associations. Unlike the special categories of religious communities—legally recognised and state-registered religious communities—non-profit associations are not identified by state bodies as "religious." Therefore, if they require legal consequences to be derived from this qualification, the circumstances must be examined by the responsible administrative or judicial body in each case.

Apart from this, every religious community—independently of its legal status—has the ability to found associations with partly religious functions (*religiöse Hilfsvereine*), primarily related to the social and charitable activities of religious communities, regardless of their legal form. According to the revenue law, benefits (reductions or exemptions) are also awarded over and above "religious" objectives to public utility and charitable purposes.

The IslamG contains some special regulations regarding Islamic associations. According to § 31 section 3 of the IslamG, associations whose objective is the dissemination of religious doctrine of a Religious Society, which already existed on the date the Act came into force, are to be dissolved by decision of the Federal Minister of the Interior if the association's purpose has not been adapted to fit the requirements of this Act. Therefore, associations have to modify their aims in good time so that they no longer include the dissemination of religious doctrine. If the purpose of the association is converted into

35 BGBl. I Nr. 66/2002 as amended BGBl. I Nr. 32/2018.

36 Cf. Tichy, Heinz, "Religiöse Gemeinschaften nach dem Vereinsgesetz 2002", in *Österreichisches Archiv für Recht und Religion*, vol. 51 (2004), pp. 379–397.

activities such as social and/or cultural activities, or the maintenance or establishment of a place of worship, the association may continue to exist.

This provision in § 31 section 3 could cause further legal problems. The doctrine of the existing Islamic Religious Society in Austria covers the entirety of the Islamic law schools, according to the concept of the eight *madhāhib* recognised by the global Islamic community.[37] Therefore, all Islamic associations, apart from the Islamic Religious Society in Austria relying on the mainstream Islam of the eight *madhāhib*, must actually be dissolved.

In regard to the (Islamic) Alevite Religious Society, the rewording with omissions of the reference to Islam[38] caused difficulties for the Alevi associations of the "Federation of Alevi Communities in Austria," which from the beginning had refused to include any reference to Islamic roots in its name.

Altogether, § 31 section 3 raises a number of questions regarding the fundamental rights of freedom of association and freedom of religion.

37 Cf. Chapter 1, fn. 11.

38 See chapter 5.

CHAPTER 3

The Federal Act on Islamic Religious Societies

In 2015 the IslamG 1912 was replaced by the "Federal Act on the external legal relationships of Islamic Religious Societies" which was long overdue.[1] The draft law was the subject of intense political debate, which has not yet stopped, even since its coming into force. In principle, this law differs from the other special laws concerning churches and religious societies in its general concept for two reasons and moreover contains some striking peculiarities.

First of all, it is not a law concerning one single religious society but covers two different religious societies, namely, the Islamic Religious Society in Austria (*Islamische Glaubensgemeinschaft in Österreich*, IGGÖ) and the Islamic Alevite Religious Society in Austria (*Islamische Alevitische Glaubensgemeinschaft in Österreich*, IAGÖ). This inclusion of the IAGÖ in the IslamG, which was mainly based on someone's self-designation as "Islamic,"[2] has been widely criticised because it disregards the fundamental differences between Islam and Alevism.[3] Fundamental problems related to the inclusion of an Alevi group in the IslamG, especially given the existence of another Alevi group, which does not want to be treated as Muslim and therefore, according to the IslamG, has not hitherto been solved.[4]

1 See Gartner-Müller, Barbara, "Die Islamische Glaubensgemeinschaft und das Ausschließlichkeitsrecht der gesetzlich anerkannten Kirchen und Religionsgesellschaften", in *Österreichisches Archiv für Recht und Religion*, vol. 59 (2012), pp. 251–283; Schima, Stefan, "Das Islamgesetz im Kontext des österreichischen Religionsrechts", in *Österreichisches Archiv für Recht und Religion*, vol. 59 (2012), pp. 225–250; Potz, Richard, and Schinkele, Brigitte, "Die Genese des österreichischen Islamgesetzes 2015", in *Österreichisches Archiv für Recht und Religion*, vol. 62 (2015), pp. 303–385.

2 Meanwhile the Islamic Alevite Religious Society has changed its name to "Alevitische Glaubensgemeinschaft in Österreich (ALEVI)". This renaming is remarkable and should be critically questioned because the reference to its Islamic roots has been essential for this group in the procedure of registration and in its inclusion in the IslamG 2015, cf. Potz, Richard, and Schinkele, Brigitte, "Eintragung bzw gesetzliche Anerkennung alevitischer Gruppen in Österreich", in *Österreichisches Archiv für Recht und Religion*, vol. 58 (2011), pp. 137–155.

3 See Sökefeld, Martin, "Sind Aleviten Muslime? Die alevitische Debatte über das Verhältnis von Alevitentum und Islam in Deutschland", in Sökefeld, Martin (ed.), *Aleviten in Deutschland. Identitätsprozesse einer Religionsgemeinschaft in der Diaspora*, Bielefeld: Transcript, 2008, pp. 195–218.

4 Cf. Hammer, Stefan, "Die Aleviten im österreichischen Religionsrecht—ein Kampf um Anerkennung. Der schwere Abschied vom Ausschließlichkeitsgrundsatz", in *Österreichisches Archiv für Recht und Religion*, vol. 65 (2018), pp. 1–17.

Secondly, it is a law which regulates not only the external legal relationships of an existing religious society but also the preconditions for the legal recognition of further Islamic religious societies. This concept is reflected in the structure of the law. The first part deals with the general legal position of Islamic religious societies and the prerequisites for the legal recognition of further Islamic religious societies. The second part includes provisions concerning Islamic religious societies. The third and fourth parts regulate the rights and obligations of the existing IGGÖ and, correspondingly, the IAGÖ. The fifth part deals with the "interaction of the religious societies and the state" in the usual way, and the sixth part—"final provisions"—includes *inter alia* the transitional rules for the two existing religious societies.

As for the specific content of the law, the wording of § 2 section 2 brings a remarkable formulation as a kind of programmatic statement, which is not found in any other special law for a recognised religious society and has triggered quite fundamental discussion. The first and second sentences, at first, repeat the phrasing of the IslamG 1912, stating that "Islamic religious societies enjoy the same legal protection as other recognised religious societies. Their teachings, institutions and customs enjoy the same legal protection, provided that they do not contradict legal regulations." The third sentence, however, is new and reads as follows: "Religious societies, congregations (*Kultusgemeinde*) or other subdivisions as well as their members may not rely on internal religious rules or teachings with respect to their duty to observe general norms of the state, unless the applicable state law provides for such a possibility in the respective case."

§ 6 section 1 of the IslamG outlines the issues the constitution of an Islamic Religious Society must deal with within the framework of the society's "internal affairs" in order to attain legal force within the sphere of the state. This list corresponds to the respective provisions in other special laws; however, it contains a significant supplement regarding the submission of its doctrine, explicitly requiring a text outlining the essential sources of faith (Qur'an) (no. 5).[5]

5 The submission of the 'doctrine, including a text of the essential sources of faith (Qur'an) in the German language' gives rise to numerous problems. The requirement of a virtually authentic text of the Qur'an in German cannot be justified, either in terms of religious science or in terms of the law on religion. Such a suggestion does not take into account the complex processes involved in interpretation of religious sources which apply in general to Holy Scriptures of revealed religions. The complexity of a translation of the Qur'an particularly calls for a detailed commentary. From the perspective of law on religion it is questionable that the explanatory notes to the bill try to legitimate the required submission of the Qur'an in the German language primarily on the grounds that the doctrine of an applicant religious society must be distinguishable from the teachings of already existing and legally recog-

§ 6 section 2 of the IslamG requires that the financial means for customary activities aimed at satisfying the religious needs of members must be obtained by the Religious Society, its cultus communities, or their members from within the country. In particular, the employment of foreign public servants in the service of religious societies and cultus communities as employees, clergy, pastors or officials is in any case prohibited by law, regardless of who pays them. This should serve the legitimate aim of preserving the independence of cultus communities from governmental influence on the part of national and foreign governments.

Cultus communities are autonomous bodies with legal personality under public law (§ 8 IslamG). They must satisfy the religious needs of their members and provide for the necessary facilities to accomplish these tasks. Every congregation requires a statute, which must deal with a number of specific issues in order to acquire legal force within the sphere of the state, and this corresponds essentially to the respective requirements of other special laws. Cultus communities may establish and administer institutions and facilities in order to fulfil their tasks. If such institutions are given legal personality by the internal law of the Religious Society, in accordance with § 23 section 4 of the IslamG they may also obtain legal status under public law by the Religious Society notifying the competent Minister.

According to Article 19 of the constitution of the IGGÖ,[6] the existence of a cultus community and its capacity for economic self-preservation are considered to be assured if it operates at least ten mosque facilities and has at least 1,000 members at the time of foundation.

As a measure of state supervision the possibility of appointing a curator is provided for (§ 29 of the IslamG).[7] If the length of function of organs authorised for external representation of the religious society or of a cultus community exceeds at least six months or if those organs are unable to act for other reasons, the state authority must invite the religious society or the cultus community within a period of at least one and at most six months to provide for elections or restore the ability to act in another way, laid down in the constitution or the statutes. If the religious society or the cultus community does not comply with this obligation and neither the religious society nor the cultus community has

nised religious societies and state-registered religious denominational communities. There are assessments at issue which evidently demand too much of a state which is neutral in religious matters.

6 See chapter 4.3.

7 This regulation follows the example of the IsraelitenG 2012 (fn. 21).

brought in a motion to appoint a curator to the competent court, the Federal Minister must submit such a request.

Bundesgesetz über die äußeren Rechtsverhältnisse islamischer Religionsgesellschaften—Islamgesetz 2015
BGBl. I Nr. 39/2015
1. Abschnitt—*Rechtsstellung*

§ 1—*Körperschaft öffentlichen Rechts*

Islamische Religionsgesellschaften in Österreich sind anerkannte Religionsgesellschaften im Sinne des Artikels 15 des Staatsgrundgesetzes über die allgemeinen Rechte der Staatsbürger. Sie sind Körperschaften des öffentlichen Rechts.

§ 2—*Selbstständigkeit*

(1) Islamische Religionsgesellschaften ordnen und verwalten ihre inneren Angelegenheiten selbständig. Sie sind in Bekenntnis und Lehre frei und haben das Recht der öffentlichen Religionsausübung.
(2) Islamische Religionsgesellschaften genießen denselben gesetzlichen Schutz wie andere gesetzlich anerkannte Religionsgesellschaften. Auch ihre Lehren, Einrichtungen und Gebräuche genießen diesen Schutz, sofern sie nicht mit gesetzlichen Regelungen in Widerspruch stehen. Religionsgesellschaften, Kultusgemeinden oder andere Untergliederungen sowie ihre Mitglieder können sich gegenüber der Pflicht zur Einhaltung allgemeiner staatlicher Normen nicht auf innerreligionsgesellschaftliche Regelungen oder die Lehre berufen, sofern das im jeweiligen Fall anzuwendende staatliche Recht nicht eine solche Möglichkeit vorsieht.

§ 3—*Erwerb der Rechtspersönlichkeit*

(1) Islamische Religionsgesellschaften erwerben die Rechtspersönlichkeit nach diesem Bundesgesetz auf Antrag durch Verordnung des Bundeskanzlers. Die Verordnung hat zu enthalten mit welchen Maßgaben Bestimmungen des 3. bzw. 4. Abschnittes auf die Religionsgesellschaft Anwendung finden. Der Lauf der Frist nach § 8 VwGVG wird durch die Zeit für eine allfällige Ergänzung des Antrages und für ein allfälliges Parteiengehör vom Zeitpunkt des Absendens des Verbesserungsauftrages oder der

Einladung zum Parteiengehör bis zum Einlangen der Ergänzung oder der Stellungnahme oder des Ablaufes der dafür festgesetzten Frist gehemmt.
(2) Der Bundeskanzler hat das Einlangen von Anträgen gemäß Abs. 1 im Internet auf einer für den Bereich „Kultusamt" einzurichtenden Homepage öffentlich zugänglich zu machen.
(3) Über den Erwerb der Rechtspersönlichkeit ist ein Bescheid zu erlassen, der den Namen der Islamischen Religionsgesellschaft sowie die nach außen vertretungsbefugten Organe in allgemeiner Bezeichnung zu enthalten hat.
(4) Mit dem Erwerb der Rechtspersönlichkeit nach Abs. 3 sind jene Vereine aufzulösen, deren Zweck in der Verbreitung der Religionslehre der betreffenden Religionsgesellschaft besteht.
(5) Wird eine islamische Religionsgesellschaft unter Auflösung eines Vereines, der der Unterstützung des betreffenden religiösen Bekenntnisses dient, neu gebildet, so ist abgabenrechtlich von einem bloßen Wechsel der Rechtsform und weiterem Fortbestehen ein und desselben Steuerpflichtigen (Rechtsträgers) auszugehen.

§ 4—*Voraussetzungen für den Erwerb der Rechtsstellung*

(1) Eine Islamische Religionsgesellschaft bedarf für den Erwerb der Rechtspersönlichkeit nach diesem Bundesgesetz eines gesicherten dauerhaften Bestandes und der wirtschaftlichen Selbsterhaltungsfähigkeit. Der gesicherte dauerhafte Bestand ist gegeben, wenn der Antragsteller eine staatlich eingetragene religiöse Bekenntnisgemeinschaft ist und über eine Anzahl an Angehörigen von mindestens 2 vT der Bevölkerung Österreichs nach der letzten Volkszählung verfügt. Den Nachweis hat der Antragsteller zu erbringen.
(2) Einnahmen und Vermögen dürfen ausschließlich für religiöse Zwecke, wozu auch in der religiösen Zielsetzung begründete gemeinnützige und mildtätige Zwecke zählen, verwendet werden.
(3) Es muss eine positive Grundeinstellung gegenüber Gesellschaft und Staat bestehen.
(4) Es darf keine gesetzwidrige Störung des Verhältnisses zu den bestehenden gesetzlich anerkannten Kirchen und Religionsgesellschaften sowie sonstigen Religionsgemeinschaften bestehen.

§ 5—*Versagung und Aufhebung der Rechtspersönlichkeit*

(1) Der Bundeskanzler hat den Erwerb der Rechtspersönlichkeit zu versagen, wenn
1. dies im Hinblick auf die Lehre oder deren Anwendung zum Schutz der in einer demokratischen Gesellschaft gegebenen Interessen der öffentlichen Sicherheit, der öffentlichen Ordnung, Gesundheit und Moral oder zum Schutz der Rechte und Freiheiten anderer notwendig ist; dies ist insbesondere bei Aufforderung zu einem mit Strafe bedrohten gesetzwidrigen Verhalten, bei einer Behinderung der psychischen Entwicklung von Heranwachsenden, bei Verletzung der psychischen Integrität und bei Anwendung psychotherapeutischer Methoden, insbesondere zum Zwecke der Glaubensvermittlung gegeben,
2. eine Voraussetzung nach § 4 fehlt,
3. die Verfassung dem § 6 nicht entspricht.
(2) Die Bundesregierung hat die Anerkennung der Religionsgesellschaft mit Verordnung, der Bundeskanzler die Rechtspersönlichkeit einer Kultusgemeinde mit Bescheid aufzuheben, wenn
1. eine für den Erwerb der Rechtsstellung maßgebliche Voraussetzung nach § 4, außer der Anzahl an Angehörigen, bzw. § 8 nicht mehr vorliegt,
2. ein Versagungsgrund gemäß Abs. 1 vorliegt, sofern trotz Aufforderung zur Abstellung des Aberkennungsgrundes dieser fortbesteht,
3. ein verfassungswidriges oder statutenwidriges Verhalten trotz Aufforderung zur Abstellung fortbesteht, oder
4. mit der Anerkennung verbundene Pflichten trotz Aufforderung nicht erfüllt werden.
(3) Nach der Kundmachung der Verordnung, mit welcher die Aufhebung der Anerkennung der Rechtspersönlichkeit erfolgte, ist binnen drei Werktagen ein Feststellungsbescheid über die Gründe zu erlassen, der den Namen der Religionsgesellschaft und die zuletzt zur Außenvertretung befugten Organe zu enthalten hat und an diese zuzustellen ist.
(4) Die Versagung oder Aufhebung der Rechtsstellung ist im Internet auf einer für den Bereich „Kultusamt" einzurichtenden Homepage öffentlich zugänglich zu machen.

2. Abschnitt—*Aufbau und Aufgaben*

§ 6—*Verfassungen islamischer Religionsgesellschaften*

(1) Eine im Rahmen der inneren Angelegenheiten erstellte Verfassung einer islamischen Religionsgesellschaft hat, um die Wirkung für den staatlichen Bereich sicherzustellen, folgende Angaben in der Amtssprache zu enthalten:
1. Name und Kurzbezeichnung, wobei die Religionsgesellschaft klar erkennbar und eine Verwechslung mit anderen Kirchen oder Religionsgesellschaften, Vereinen, Einrichtungen oder anderen Rechtsformen ausgeschlossen sein muss;
2. Sitz der Religionsgesellschaft;
3. Erwerb und Verlust der Mitgliedschaft;
4. Rechte und Pflichten der Mitglieder;
5. Darstellung der Lehre, einschließlich eines Textes der wesentlichen Glaubensquellen (Koran), die sich von bestehenden gesetzlich anerkannten Religionsgesellschaften, Bekenntnisgemeinschaften oder Religionsgesellschaften unterscheiden müssen;
6. innere Organisation, wobei zumindest Kultusgemeinden vorzusehen sind;
7. angemessene Berücksichtigung aller innerhalb der Religionsgesellschaft bestehenden Traditionen;
8. Art der Bestellung, Dauer der Funktionsperiode und Abberufung der Organe;
9. Art der Besorgung des Religionsunterrichts und die Aufsicht über diesen;
10. Aufbringung der Mittel, deren Verwaltung und die Rechnungslegung;
11. Schlichtung von Streitigkeiten innerhalb der Religionsgesellschaft;
12. Erzeugung und Änderung der Verfassung.
(2) Die Aufbringung der Mittel für die gewöhnliche Tätigkeit zur Befriedigung der religiösen Bedürfnisse ihrer Mitglieder hat durch die Religionsgesellschaft, die Kultusgemeinden bzw. ihre Mitglieder im Inland zu erfolgen.

Case Law[8]

8 See chapter 9.2.

§ 7—*Aufgaben einer Religionsgesellschaft*

Einer Religionsgesellschaft obliegen insbesondere
1. die Vertretung der Interessen ihrer Mitglieder, soweit sie über den Wirkungsbereich einer Kultusgemeinde hinausreichen; sie ist religionsgesellschaftliche Oberbehörde;
2. die Vorlage der Verfassung der Religionsgesellschaft und von Statuten der Kultusgemeinden, deren Änderungen sowie Änderungen in der Zusammensetzung der Organe an den Bundeskanzler;
3. die Vorlage von nach innerreligionsgesellschaftlichem Recht mit Rechtspersönlichkeit ausgestatteten Einrichtungen für die Erlangung der Rechtspersönlichkeit auch für den staatlichen Bereich, deren vertretungsbefugten Organe und Organwalter sowie deren Änderungen an den Bundeskanzler.

§ 8—*Kultusgemeinden*

(1) Kultusgemeinden sind Teile einer islamischen Religionsgesellschaft, die zugleich selbstständige Körperschaften öffentlichen Rechts sind. Sie haben für die Befriedigung der religiösen Bedürfnisse ihrer Mitglieder und für die Bereitstellung der dafür erforderlichen Einrichtungen zu sorgen.
(2) Die Kultusgemeinden können zur Erfüllung der in Abs. 1 genannten Aufgaben Einrichtungen gründen, führen oder bestehende Einrichtungen zu solchen der Kultusgemeinde erklären. Gemeinsame Einrichtungen mehrerer Kultusgemeinden können nur im allseitigen Einvernehmen und mit Zustimmung der Religionsgesellschaft gegründet werden.
(3) Kultusgemeinden können nur gegründet werden, wenn deren Bestand und wirtschaftliche Selbsterhaltungsfähigkeit gesichert ist und die Religionsgesellschaft der Gründung zustimmt.
(4) Jede Kultusgemeinde hat sich ein Statut zu geben, welches um die Wirkung für den staatlichen Bereich sicher zu stellen
1. Name und eine Kurzbezeichnung der Kultusgemeinde, wobei die Religionsgesellschaft klar erkennbar und eine Verwechslung mit anderen Kirchen oder Religionsgesellschaften, Vereinen, Einrichtungen, Kultusgemeinden oder anderen Rechtsformen ausgeschlossen sein muss,
2. den Sitz der Kultusgemeinde,
3. Bestimmungen über Erwerb und Verlust der Mitgliedschaft,
4. die Rechte und Pflichten der Mitglieder,

5. Regelungen über die innere Organisation, insbesondere über ein Mitgliederverzeichnis,
6. Regelungen über die Art der Bestellung, Dauer der Funktionsperiode und Abberufung der Organe,
7. Regelungen über die Aufbringung der Mittel, deren Verwaltung und über die Rechnungslegung,
8. Regelungen über die Schlichtung von Streitigkeiten innerhalb der Kultusgemeinden, und
9. Regelungen über die Erzeugung und Änderung des Statuts
enthalten muss.
(5) Bei Auflösung einer Kultusgemeinde haben die zuletzt tätigen Organe im Einvernehmen mit der Religionsgesellschaft über das Vermögen zu bestimmen.

3. Abschnitt—*Rechte und Pflichten der „Islamischen Glaubensgemeinschaft in Österreich"*

§ 9—*Namensrecht und Schutz der religiösen Bezeichnungen*

(1) Die Religionsgesellschaft hat das Recht, einen Namen im Rahmen der in § 6 Abs. 1 Z 1 genannten Grenzen zu wählen.
(2) Die Namen der Religionsgesellschaft und der Kultusgemeinden sowie alle daraus abgeleiteten Begriffe dürfen nur mit Zustimmung der Religionsgesellschaft oder Kultusgemeinde verwendet werden.
(3) Bezeichnungen, die geeignet sind gegenüber außenstehenden Dritten den Eindruck einer rechtlichen Verbindung zu einzelnen Einrichtungen der Religionsgesellschaft, einer Kultusgemeinde oder ähnlicher Institutionen außerhalb Österreichs herzustellen, dürfen nur mit Zustimmung der Religionsgesellschaft verwendet werden.
(4) Bei Verstößen gegen diese Bestimmungen haben die Religionsgesellschaft und jede betroffene Kultusgemeinde das Recht, einen Antrag auf Einleitung eines Verfahrens zur Beendigung des rechtswidrigen Zustandes an den Bundeskanzler zu stellen, wenn nicht strafgesetzliche Bestimmungen anzuwenden sind. Über den Antrag ist binnen vier Wochen zu entscheiden.

§ 10—*Begutachtungsrecht*

(1) Die Religionsgesellschaft ist berechtigt, den Organen der Gesetzgebung und Verwaltung auf allen Ebenen Gutachten, Stellungnahmen, Be-

richte und Vorschläge über Angelegenheiten, die gesetzlich anerkannte Kirchen und Religionsgesellschaften betreffen, zu übermitteln.
(2) Rechtsetzende Maßnahmen, die die äußeren Rechtsverhältnisse der Religionsgesellschaft betreffen, sind vor ihrer Vorlage, Verordnungen vor ihrer Erlassung, der Religionsgesellschaft unter Gewährung einer angemessenen Frist zur Stellungnahme zu übermitteln.

§ 11—*Recht auf religiöse Betreuung in besonderen Einrichtungen und Jugenderziehung*

(1) Die Religionsgesellschaft hat das Recht, ihre Mitglieder, die
1. Angehörige des Bundesheeres sind oder
2. sich in gerichtlicher oder verwaltungsbehördlicher Haft befinden oder
3. in öffentlichen Krankenanstalten, Versorgungs-, Pflege- oder ähnlichen Anstalten untergebracht sind,
in religiöser Hinsicht zu betreuen.
(2) Zur Besorgung der Angelegenheiten des Abs. 1 kommen nur Personen in Betracht, die aufgrund ihrer Ausbildung und ihres Lebensmittelpunktes in Österreich fachlich und persönlich dafür geeignet sind. Sie unterstehen in allen konfessionellen Belangen der Religionsgesellschaft, in allen anderen Angelegenheiten der jeweils zuständigen Leitung für die Einrichtung. Die fachliche Eignung liegt nur dann vor, wenn ein Abschluss eines Studiums gemäß § 24 oder eine gleichwertige Qualifikation vorliegt. Die persönliche Eignung erfordert mindestens 3 Jahre einschlägige Berufserfahrung und Deutschkenntnisse auf dem Niveau der Reifeprüfung. Weiters ist eine Ermächtigung durch die Religionsgesellschaft erforderlich.
(3) Der für die Besorgung der Angelegenheiten nach Abs. 1 Z 1 erforderliche Sach- und Personalaufwand ist vom Bund zu tragen.
(4) Die Religionsgesellschaft und ihre Mitglieder sind berechtigt, Kinder und Jugendliche durch alle traditionellen Bräuche zu führen und entsprechend den religiösen Geboten zu erziehen.

§ 12—*Speisevorschriften*

(1) Die Religionsgesellschaft hat das Recht, in Österreich die Herstellung von Fleischprodukten und anderen Nahrungsmitteln gemäß ihren innerreligionsgesellschaftlichen Vorschriften zu organisieren.
(2) Bei der Verpflegung von Mitgliedern der Religionsgesellschaft beim Bundesheer, in Haftanstalten, öffentlichen Krankenanstalten, Versor-

gungs-, Pflege- oder ähnlichen Anstalten sowie öffentlichen Schulen ist auf die innerreligionsgesellschaftlichen Speisegebote Rücksicht zu nehmen.

§ 13—*Feiertage*

(1) Feiertagen und der Zeit des Freitagsgebetes wird der Schutz des Staates gewährleistet. Ihre Termine richten sich nach dem islamischen Kalender. Die Tage beginnen mit Sonnenuntergang und dauern bis Sonnenuntergang des folgenden Tages. Die Gebetszeit ist am Freitag von 12.00 Uhr bis 14.00 Uhr.
(2) Feiertage sind
a) Ramadanfest (3 Tage)
b) Pilger-Opferfest (4 Tage)
c) Aschura (1 Tag).
(3) An den in Abs. 2 bezeichneten Tagen und während des Freitagsgebetes sind in der Nähe von Kultstätten und sonstigen Kultusgemeinden zu gottesdienstlichen Zwecken dienenden Räumen und Gebäuden alle vermeidbaren, Lärm erregenden Handlungen, die eine Beeinträchtigung der Feier zur Folge haben könnten, sowie öffentliche Versammlungen, Auf- und Umzüge, untersagt.

§ 14—*Abberufung von Funktionsträgern und -trägerinnen*

Die Religionsgesellschaft und die Kultusgemeinden haben Funktionsträger und -trägerinnen, einschließlich religiöser Funktionsträger und trägerinnen, die durch ein inländisches Gericht wegen einer oder mehrerer mit Vorsatz begangener strafbarer Handlungen zu einer mehr als einjährigen Freiheitsstrafe rechtskräftig verurteilt worden sind oder durch ihr Verhalten die öffentliche Sicherheit, Ordnung, Gesundheit und Moral oder die Rechte und Freiheiten anderer nachhaltig gefährden, ihrer Funktionen zu entheben.

§ 15—*Friedhöfe*

(1) Friedhöfe bzw. Friedhofsabteilungen sind auf Dauer angelegt. Ihre Auflösung oder Schließung sowie Enterdigungen einzelner Grabstellen sind unzulässig. Ausnahmen bedürfen der Zustimmung der religionsgesellschaftlichen Oberbehörde.
(2) Bestattungen auf Friedhöfen bzw. Friedhofsabteilungen dürfen nur

mit Zustimmung der religionsgesellschaftlichen Oberbehörde vorgenommen werden.

4. Abschnitt—*Rechte und Pflichten der „Islamischen Alevitischen Glaubensgemeinschaft in Österreich“*

§ 16—*Namensrecht und Schutz der religiösen Bezeichnungen*

(1) Die Religionsgesellschaft hat das Recht, einen Namen im Rahmen der in § 6 Abs. 1 Z 1 genannten Grenzen zu wählen.
(2) Die Namen der Religionsgesellschaft und der Kultusgemeinden sowie alle daraus abgeleiteten Begriffe dürfen nur mit Zustimmung der Religionsgesellschaft oder Kultusgemeinde verwendet werden.
(3) Bezeichnungen, die geeignet sind gegenüber außenstehenden Dritten den Eindruck einer rechtlichen Verbindung zu einzelnen Einrichtungen einer Religionsgesellschaft, einer Kultusgemeinde oder ähnlicher Institutionen außerhalb Österreichs herzustellen, dürfen nur mit Zustimmung der Religionsgesellschaft verwendet werden.
(4) Bei Verstößen gegen diese Bestimmungen haben die Religionsgesellschaft und jede betroffene Kultusgemeinde das Recht, einen Antrag auf Einleitung eines Verfahrens zur Beendigung des rechtswidrigen Zustandes an den Bundeskanzler zu stellen, wenn nicht strafgesetzliche Bestimmungen anzuwenden sind. Über den Antrag ist binnen vier Wochen zu entscheiden.

§ 17—*Begutachtungsrecht*

(1) Die Religionsgesellschaft ist berechtigt, den Organen der Gesetzgebung und Verwaltung auf allen Ebenen Gutachten, Stellungnahmen, Berichte und Vorschläge über Angelegenheiten, die gesetzlich anerkannte Kirchen und Religionsgesellschaften betreffen, zu übermitteln.
(2) Rechtsetzende Maßnahmen, die die äußeren Rechtsverhältnisse der Religionsgesellschaft betreffen, sind vor ihrer Vorlage, Verordnungen vor ihrer Erlassung, der Religionsgesellschaft unter Gewährung einer angemessenen Frist zur Stellungnahme zu übermitteln.

§ 18—*Recht auf religiöse Betreuung in besonderen Einrichtungen und Jugenderziehung*

(1) Die Religionsgesellschaft hat das Recht, ihre Mitglieder, die
1. Angehörige des Bundesheeres sind oder
2. sich in gerichtlicher oder verwaltungsbehördlicher Haft befinden oder
3. in öffentlichen Krankenanstalten, Versorgungs-, Pflege- oder ähnlichen Anstalten untergebracht sind,
in religiöser Hinsicht zu betreuen.
(2) Zur Besorgung der Angelegenheiten des Abs. 1 kommen nur Personen, insbesondere Dedes, Babas und Anas, in Betracht, die aufgrund ihrer Ausbildung und ihres Lebensmittelpunktes in Österreich fachlich und persönlich dafür geeignet sind. Sie unterstehen in allen konfessionellen Belangen der Religionsgesellschaft, in allen anderen Angelegenheiten der jeweils zuständigen Leitung für die Einrichtung. Die fachliche Eignung liegt nur dann vor, wenn ein Abschluss eines Studiums gemäß § 24 oder eine gleichwertige Qualifikation vorliegt. Die persönliche Eignung erfordert mindestens 3 Jahre einschlägige Berufserfahrung und Deutschkenntnisse auf dem Niveau der Reifeprüfung. Weiters ist eine Ermächtigung durch die Religionsgesellschaft erforderlich.
(3) Der für die Besorgung der Angelegenheiten nach Abs. 1 Z 1 erforderliche Sach- und Personalaufwand ist vom Bund zu tragen.
(4) Die Religionsgesellschaft und ihre Mitglieder sind berechtigt, Kinder und Jugendliche durch alle traditionellen Bräuche zu führen und entsprechend den religiösen Geboten zu erziehen.

§ 19—*Speisevorschriften*

(1) Die Religionsgesellschaft hat das Recht, in Österreich die Herstellung von Fleischprodukten und anderen Nahrungsmitteln gemäß ihren innerreligionsgesellschaftlichen Vorschriften zu organisieren.
(2) Bei der Verpflegung von Mitgliedern der Religionsgesellschaft beim Bundesheer, in Haftanstalten, öffentlichen Krankenanstalten, Versorgungs-, Pflege- oder ähnlichen Anstalten sowie öffentlichen Schulen ist auf die innerreligionsgesellschaftlichen Speisegebote Rücksicht zu nehmen.

§ 20—*Feiertage*

(1) Feiertagen und den Gottesdiensten (donnerstäglicher Cem-Gottesdienst, Lokma-Tage) wird der Schutz des Staates gewährleistet. Die Termine der Feiertage richten sich nach dem islamischen Kalender. Die Tage beginnen mit Sonnenuntergang und dauern bis Sonnenuntergang des folgenden Tages.
(2) Feiertage sind
a) Fasten- und Feiertage in Gedenken des Heiligen Hizir (3 Tage)
b) Geburt des Heiligen Ali (1 Tag)
c) Opferfest (4 Tage)
d) Ausrufung Alis als Nachfolger Mohammeds (1 Tag)
e) Asure (1 Tag)
(3) An den in Abs. 2 bezeichneten Tagen bzw. während der Gottesdienste sind in der Nähe von Kultstätten und sonstigen Kultusgemeinden zu gottesdienstlichen Zwecken dienenden Räumen und Gebäuden alle vermeidbaren, Lärm erregenden Handlungen, die eine Beeinträchtigung der Feier zur Folge haben könnten, sowie öffentliche Versammlungen, Auf- und Umzüge, untersagt.

§ 21—*Abberufung von Funktionsträgern und -trägerinnen*

Eine Religionsgesellschaft und die Kultusgemeinden haben Funktionsträger und -trägerinnen, einschließlich religiöser Funktionsträger und trägerinnen, die durch ein inländisches Gericht wegen einer oder mehrerer mit Vorsatz begangener strafbarer Handlungen zu einer mehr als einjährigen Freiheitsstrafe rechtskräftig verurteilt worden sind oder durch ihr Verhalten die öffentliche Sicherheit, Ordnung, Gesundheit und Moral oder die Rechte und Freiheiten anderer nachhaltig gefährden, ihrer Funktionen zu entheben.

§ 22—*Friedhöfe*

(1) Friedhöfe bzw. Friedhofsabteilungen sind auf Dauer angelegt. Ihre Auflösung oder Schließung sowie Enterdigungen einzelner Grabstellen sind unzulässig. Ausnahmen bedürfen der Zustimmung der religionsgesellschaftlichen Oberbehörde.
(2) Bestattungen auf Friedhöfen bzw. Friedhofsabteilungen dürfen nur mit Zustimmung der religionsgesellschaftlichen Oberbehörde vorgenommen werden.

5. Abschnitt—*Zusammenwirken von Religionsgesellschaften und Staat*

§ 23—*Rechtswirksamkeit innerreligionsgesellschaftlicher Entscheidungen*

(1) Die Verfassung einer Religionsgesellschaft, die Statuten von Kultusgemeinden sowie in diesen begründete Verfahrensordnungen, insbesondere Kultusumlagenordnung und Wahlordnung, und deren Änderungen bedürfen zu ihrer Gültigkeit der Genehmigung des Bundeskanzlers.
(2) Die aufgrund der Verfassung und der Statuten zur Außenvertretung befugten Organe sowie die Religionsdienerinnen und -diener sind dem Bundeskanzler unverzüglich nach der Wahl bzw. Bestellung von der Religionsgesellschaft (§ 7 Z 2) zur Kenntnis zu bringen.
(3) Änderungen von Regelungen gemäß Abs. 1 und Bestellungen von vertretungsbefugten Organen treten erst mit dem Tag der Bestätigung durch den Bundeskanzler in Kraft. Sie sind von diesem im Internet auf einer für den Bereich „Kultusamt" einzurichtenden Homepage öffentlich zugänglich zu machen.
(4) Nach innerreligionsgesellschaftlichem Recht mit Rechtspersönlichkeit ausgestattete Einrichtungen erlangen für den staatlichen Bereich Rechtspersönlichkeit des öffentlichen Rechts mit dem Tag des Einlangens der durch die Religionsgesellschaft ausgefertigten Anzeige beim Bundeskanzler, der das Einlangen schriftlich zu bestätigen hat. Die Anzeige muss den Wirkungsbereich der Rechtsperson und jene Personen, welche sie nach außen vertreten enthalten.[9]

§ 24—*Theologische Studien*

(1) Der Bund hat ab dem 1. Jänner 2016 zum Zwecke der theologischen Forschung und Lehre und für die wissenschaftliche Heranbildung des geistlichen Nachwuchses islamischer Religionsgesellschaften den Bestand einer theologischen Ausbildung an der Universität Wien zu erhalten. Für diese sind insgesamt bis zu sechs Stellen für Lehrpersonal vorzusehen.
(2) Für jede Religionsgesellschaft nach diesem Bundesgesetz ist ein eigener Zweig im Studium vorzusehen.

9 According to § 23 section 4 of the IslamG, Islamic Religious Societies have the ability to extend their public-law status to institutions such as foundations, social and charitable facilities. Regardless of this special legal provision, institutions of religious communities may use all other legal forms under private law.

(3) Als Lehrpersonal gemäß Abs. 1 kommen Universitätsprofessorinnen und Universitätsprofessoren, Universitätsdozentinnen und Universitätsdozenten, Privatdozentinnen und Privatdozenten sowie assoziierte Professorinnen und Professoren im Sinne des Kollektivvertrages für die ArbeitnehmerInnen der Universitäten gemäß §108 Abs. 3 Universitätsgesetz in Betracht.
(4) Vor der Besetzung von Stellen nach Abs. 1 ist mit den Religionsgesellschaften in Fühlungnahme über die in Aussicht genommene Person zu treten, wobei im theologischen Kernbereich darauf Bedacht zu nehmen ist, dass es sich um Anhänger der in der jeweiligen nach diesem Bundesgesetz anerkannten Religionsgesellschaft vertretenen Glaubenslehre (Rechtsschule, Glaubensströmung) handelt.

Anzeige- und Meldeverpflichtungen

§ 25—*Anzeige- und Meldeverpflichtungen*

Die Religionsgesellschaft und die Republik sind verpflichtet, über Ereignisse, die eine Angelegenheit dieses Bundesgesetzes berühren, den jeweils anderen zu informieren. Dies gilt insbesondere für die Einleitung und Beendigung von Verfahren, sowie die Verhängung von Haft für den in den §§14 und 21 genannten Personenkreis, sowie für innerreligionsgesellschaftliche Rechtsmittel gegen Wahlen in der Religionsgesellschaft oder einer Kultusgemeinde.

§ 26—*Schutz der Amtsverschwiegenheit*

(1) Religiöse Funktionsträger dürfen als Zeugen, unbeschadet der sonst hiefür geltenden Vorschriften, nicht in Ansehung dessen vernommen werden, was ihnen unter dem Siegel der Amtsverschwiegenheit anvertraut wurde.
(2) Abs. 1 gilt auch für die Vernehmung als Auskunftspersonen oder Parteien im zivilgerichtlichen Verfahren.

§ 27—*Untersagung von Veranstaltungen*

Die Behörde kann Versammlungen und Veranstaltungen zu Kultuszwecken untersagen, von denen eine unmittelbare Gefahr für die Interessen der öffentlichen Sicherheit, Ordnung oder Gesundheit oder der nationalen Sicherheit oder die Rechte und Freiheiten anderer ausgeht. Gefahren, die aus Anlass der Veranstaltung von Dritten ausgehen, stellen keinen Untersagungsgrund dar.

§ 28—*Wahlen*

(1) Falls außenvertretungsbefugte Organe oder Religionsdienerinnen und -diener durch Wahl bestimmt werden, muss der Wahlvorgang entweder in der Verfassung, den Statuten oder einer Wahlordnung so ausreichend bestimmt sein, dass eine Überprüfung des Wahlvorganges möglich ist.
(2) Falls außenvertretungsbefugte Organe oder Religionsdienerinnen und -diener durch Wahl bestimmt werden, steht jeder und jedem aktiv Wahlberechtigten oder jeder und jedem, der oder die aufgrund der Wahlregelungen gemäß Abs. 1 aktiv wahlberechtigt sein könnte, nach Erschöpfung der innerreligionsgesellschaftlichen Möglichkeiten das Recht einer Wahlaufsichtsbeschwerde an den Bundeskanzler zu.
(3) Wenn nicht binnen 14 Tagen ab Einlangen der Wahlanzeige eine Mitteilung über ein innerreligionsgesellschaftliches Rechtsmittel oder eine Beschwerde aufgrund Abs. 2 eingeht, so hat der Bundeskanzler das Wahlergebnis zur Kenntnis zu nehmen und eine Bestätigung über die Wahlanzeige auszustellen.

§ 29—*Kuratorenbestellung*

(1) Ist die Dauer der Funktionsperiode von zur Außenvertretung befugten Organen der Religionsgesellschaft oder einer Kultusgemeinde um zumindest sechs Monate überschritten oder sind diese aus anderen Gründen nicht mehr handlungsfähig, so hat die Behörde die betreffende Kultusgemeinde und die Religionsgesellschaft aufzufordern, binnen einer Frist von zumindest einem und höchstens sechs Monaten die vorgesehenen Wahlen durchzuführen oder die Handlungsfähigkeit auf andere, den Statuten oder der Verfassung entsprechende, Art wieder herzustellen.
(2) Kommt die Kultusgemeinde oder die Religionsgesellschaft dem Auftrag nicht nach und hat weder die Kultusgemeinde noch die Religionsgesellschaft einen Antrag auf Bestellung einer Kuratorin oder eines Kurators beim zuständigen Gericht eingebracht, so hat der Bundeskanzler einen solchen Antrag beim zuständigen Gericht einzubringen.

§ 30—*Durchsetzung von behördlichen Entscheidungen*

Zur Durchsetzung von Entscheidungen nach diesem Bundesgesetz kann die Behörde mit Bescheid gesetz-, verfassungs- oder statutenwidrige Beschlüsse aufheben, Geldbußen in angemessener Höhe verhängen sowie andere gesetzlich vorgesehene Mittel einsetzen.

6. Abschnitt—*Schlussbestimmungen*

§ 31—*Bestehende Religionsgesellschaften, Kultusgemeinden, Verfassungen und Statuten*

(1) Die Islamische Glaubensgemeinschaft in Österreich, BGBl. Nr. 466/1988, und die Islamische Alevitische Glaubensgemeinschaft in Österreich, BGBl. II Nr. 133/2013, sowie deren Teile mit eigener Rechtspersönlichkeit bleiben in ihrem Bestande unberührt. Sie sind Religionsgesellschaften nach § 9 bzw. § 16 dieses Bundesgesetzes. Binnen vierzehn Tagen nach Inkrafttreten dieses Bundesgesetzes sind Verordnungen gemäß § 3 Abs. 1 zu erlassen, die den Bestand als Religionsgesellschaft nach diesem Bundesgesetz mit dem Tag des Inkraftretens dieses Bundesgesetzes feststellen.
(2) Verfassungen, Statuten sowie gewählte Organe bleiben in Geltung bzw. in Funktion. Sie sind mit den Bestimmungen dieses Bundesgesetzes bis zum 31. Dezember 2015 in Einklang zu bringen. Über diese Änderungen der Verfassungen und Statuten hat der Bundeskanzler bis spätestens 1. März 2016 zu entscheiden.
(3) Vereine, deren Zweck in der Verbreitung der Religionslehre einer Religionsgesellschaft nach diesem Bundesgesetz besteht und die zum Zeitpunkt des Inkrafttretens dieses Bundesgesetzes bestehen, sind zum 1. März 2016 mit Bescheid des Bundesministers für Inneres aufzulösen, wenn der Vereinszweck nicht an die Erfordernisse dieses Gesetzes angepasst wurde.
(4) Zum Zeitpunkt des Inkrafttretens dieses Bundesgesetzes tätige religiöse Funktionsträger können in Ausnahme zu den Bestimmungen des § 6 Abs. 2 ihre Funktion bis zu einem Jahr ab Inkrafttreten dieses Bundesgesetzes weiter ausüben.

§ 32—*In- und Außerkrafttreten*

Das Gesetz tritt mit Ablauf des Tages der Kundmachung im Bundesgesetzblatt in Kraft. Mit dem Inkrafttreten dieses Bundesgesetzes tritt das Gesetz betreffend die Anerkennung der Anhänger des Islam als Religionsgesellschaft, RGBl 159/1912 idF BGBl. 144/1988 (Anm.: richtig: idF BGBl. Nr. 164/1988), zuletzt geändert durch das Bundesministeriengesetz 2014, BGBl. I Nr. 11/2014, außer Kraft.

§ 33—*Vollzugsklauseln*

Mit der Vollziehung dieses Bundesgesetzes ist der Bundeskanzler betraut, soweit aufgrund einzelner Regelungen nicht die sachliche Zuständigkeit einer Bundesministerin oder eines Bundesministers besteht.

CHAPTER 4

Islamische Glaubensgemeinschaft in Österreich (IGGÖ)

4.1 Introduction

As a legally recognised religious community, the IGGÖ has enjoyed the position of a statutory body under public law since 1979.[1] By granting them public law status, the state offers to cooperate with these religious communities which, however, also implies that they must be ready and willing to fulfill the constitutional expectations that are implicitly associated with recognition. This presupposes that the respective religious community accepts the democratic state governed by the rule of law and complies with the fundamental consensus in society.

From the very start, some tensions existing round the IGGÖ were mainly rooted in the different ethnic traditions of Muslims and/or the political developments in their countries of origin. It was in particular the claim to sole representation that had already triggered criticism within the Muslim community in the 1980s. Turkish-Muslim associations like the ATIB (*Türkisch Islamische Union in Österreich*, Turkish Islamic Union in Austria), as by far the largest group in terms of membership figures within the IGGÖ, felt underrepresented in its official organs.

An issue that has been a recurrent source of criticism was the *ex lege* membership of all Muslims of the IGGÖ in line with the model of governmental self-administration institutions, which is, however, frequently considered inadequate in the case of Islam. In this sense, the *ex lege* membership of Austrian Muslims of the IGGÖ represented a weak point that had made the Islamic Community vulnerable to criticism particularly in light of the Austrian Muslims' ethnic and theological diversity.

Not least because of such disputes, the IGGÖ started to focus on amending its charter in 2007 with a new complicated election system. During stage one of the election process, i.e. the registration of eligible voters, 124,465 individuals signed up as members according to official figures from the IGGÖ. Of these, however, only 27,095 were actually entitled to vote because they had paid the

1 See chapter 1.2.

mandatory annual membership fee, and of these only 20,485 individuals actually voted. The number of registered members may serve as an indication of the IGGÖ's reach at that time.

4.2 The Federal Act on Islamic Religious Societies

The specific rights and obligations of the existing Islamic Religious Society in Austria are formulated in Part 3 §§ 9–15 of the IslamG.[2]

4.3 The Internal Law of the Islamic Religious Society in Austria

Due to the requirements of the IslamG 2015, the IGGÖ adopted a new constitution on 16 December 2015, according to which membership of the Islamic religious community is presumed for all Muslims in Austria who have put "Islam" in the column "religion" of the state population register on the confession of religion and do not already belong to another religious society recognised by the Republic of Austria or to a registered religious community. This constitution was approved by the responsible federal minister. On 15 June 2019, an amendment was decided by the Shura Council of the IGGÖ.

Verfassung der Islamischen Glaubensgemeinschaft in Österreich vom 16. Dezember 2015[3] (VfIGGÖ)[4]
Der Bestand der Rechtspersönlichkeit der „Islamischen Glaubensgemeinschaft in Österreich" wurde als gesetzlich anerkannte Religionsgesellschaft im Sinne des Artikel 15 des Staatsgrundgesetzes 1867 über die allgemeinen Rechte der Staatsbürger mit Verordnung des Bundesministers für Kunst und Kultur, Verfassung und Medien betreffend die Feststellung des Bestandes der Islamischen Glaubensgemeinschaft in Österreich als Religionsgesellschaft, BGBl II 76/2015, gemäß § 3 Abs. 1 IslamG 2015 festgestellt. In Entsprechung des § 31 Abs. 2 Islamgesetz 2015 (Bundesgesetz

2 See chapter 3.
3 In the version of 30 June 2018.
4 http://www.derislam.at/iggo/?c=content&cssid=Verfassung&navid=228&par=100 [last accessed 8 January 2020]; see also *Österreichisches Archiv für Recht und Religion*, vol. 65 (2018), pp. 91–114. In what follows only the principal religious assignment, the membership rules and the provisions for the setting up of a cultus community are printed.

über die äußeren Rechtsverhältnisse islamischer Religionsgesellschaften) iVm § 6 leg. cit erlässt der Schurarat [...] nachstehende Verfassung [...]

III.—*Mitgliedschaft, Rechte und Pflichten, Beendigung*
Art. 3

(1) Bei allen Muslimen in Österreich,[5] welche im Melderegister bei den Angaben zum Religionsbekenntnis „Islam" angegeben haben und nicht bereits einer anderen in der Republik Österreich gesetzlich anerkannten Religionsgesellschaft oder einer eingetragenen Bekenntnisgemeinschaft angehören, wird die Mitgliedschaft bei der Islamischen Glaubensgemeinschaft vermutet. Bei dieser Angabe handelt es sich um eine deklaratorische Erklärung, welche jederzeit durch einen formlosen Widerspruch gegenüber der Islamischen Glaubensgemeinschaft entkräftet werden kann. Darüber hinaus können auch Muslime, welche nicht bereits einer anderen in der Republik Österreich gesetzlich anerkannten Religionsgesellschaft oder einer eingetragenen Bekenntnisgemeinschaft angehören, auf Antrag als Mitglieder der Islamischen Glaubensgemeinschaft in Österreich aufgenommen werden. Die Mitglieder sind über die jeweiligen Religionsgemeinden in das bei der Islamischen Glaubensgemeinschaft in Österreich geführte Mitgliederverzeichnis aufzunehmen. [...]

VI.—*Innere Organisation der Islamischen Glaubensgemeinschaft in Österreich*
...
Art. 19. Die Kultusgemeinden
...

5 The underlying understanding of Islam includes at least the eight law schools, recognised by the summit meeting of the Organisation of the Islamic Conference in December 2005 and by the International Islamic Fiqh Academy in Jeddah (see fn. 11). This would exclude the recognition of other Islamic religious societies or the registration of religious confessional communities, and even the establishment of associations from the circle of the eight law schools.

Meanwhile, however, statutes of other communities claiming in particular to represent the Twelver Shia and the Zaidites have been approved by the *Kultusamt*. The constitutions of both the Alevite faith community (see chapter 5) and the Shiite confessional community (see chapter 6.2) claim membership of Muslims belonging to these two Shiite schools of law traditionally represented in the IGGÖ.

(3) Kultusgemeinden können nur gegründet werden, wenn deren Bestand und wirtschaftliche Selbsterhaltungsfähigkeit gesichert ist und die Islamische Glaubensgemeinschaft in Österreich der Gründung zustimmt. Der Bestand einer Kultusgemeinde und die wirtschaftliche Selbsterhaltungsfähigkeit gelten als gesichert, wenn sie zumindest zehn Moscheeeinrichtungen betreibt und zum Zeitpunkt der Gründung über wenigstens 1.000 Mitglieder verfügt. Moscheeeinrichtungen sind nur jene Einrichtungen, welche die nachstehenden Kriterien erfüllen:
1. Gebetsraum für mindestens 40 Personen
2. Regelmäßiges Freitagsgebet
3. Ordentlicher Imam
4. Verbreitung der Lehre

CHAPTER 5

(Islamic) Alevi Religious Society in Austria

5.1 Alevis in Austria

On 19 March 2009 the "Cultural Association of Alevites in Vienna" (*Kulturverein der Aleviten in Wien/VAKB*), a member association of the Alevi Federation of Austria (*Föderation der Aleviten Gemeinden in Österreich/AABF*), applied for legal recognition in accordance with the IslamG 1912 as *"Islamische Alevitische Glaubensgemeinschaft in Österreich,"* and eventually for registration in accordance with the BekGG 1998 as *"Islamische Alevitische Bekenntnisgemeinschaft."* Unlike the umbrella organisation, AABF, it was important for the self-understanding of the VAKB to emphasise Alevism's Islamic roots.[1] The application was dismissed by the *Kultusamt*, which argued:

> The doctrine of the requesting community contains elements as they exist in particular in Shiite Islam, as well as contents that could not be found in any other religion; therefore, ultimately the self-assignment of the applicant to Islam is crucial. Since there is already a legally recognised religious society for the followers of Islam, namely the IGGÖ, and, after the fulfillment of the requirements of § 11 BekGG,[2] the requesting community would have to be recognised, so that there would be two legally recognised religious societies that understood themselves as Islamic, which is prohibited in the IslamG.[3]

The Constitutional Court overruled this decision.[4] The Court stated that there could be more than just one Islamic religious society or community. It pointed out that if, according to a group's self-perception, reference to Islam is essential the religiously neutral state may not prohibit the use of such part of a name. Therefore, the religiously neutral state was wrong in prohibiting the addition

1 Martin Sökefeld points out that currently two principal positions have triggered a 'fiercely led debate' within the Alevi organisations: Some understand Alevism as an independent religion; for others it definitely belongs to Islam. The author also notes a growing turning away from Islam against the background of the special recognition conditions in the—in this case German—migration society: Sökefeld, Martin (fn. 3).

2 The status of Religious Denominational Communities principally is designed as a preliminary stage for legal recognition, see Chapter 2, fn. 34.

3 According to the quotation in VfGH 1. 12., VfSlg 19.240.

4 VfGH, 1. 12. 2010, VfSlg 19.240.

of the term "Islamic" by an Alevite group if the reference to Islam was essential to the group's self-understanding. This means that henceforth a group that is not covered by the IslamG 1912 may call itself Islamic and file a petition for recognition and registration.

In a first step, the *"Islamische Alevitische Glaubensgemeinschaft in Österreich"* (IAGÖ, Islamic Alevi Community in Austria) was consequently registered according to the BekGG. The request for registration of the umbrella organization, *"Alevi Federation of Austria,"* however was rejected because of the substantial identity of doctrine and creed with those of the IAGÖ.[5] The different position in relation to Islam was not regarded as a relevant distinction by the administrative body for religious affairs, the *Kultusamt*; a view that has so far been supported in several decisions of the administrative courts.[6]

The questions concerning the legal treatment of the other Alevi group—which does not consider a reference to Islam as pivotal—however has not yet been definitively clarified. The situation was furthermore complicated because the IAGÖ, since the urgently required inclusion in the IslamG 2015,[7] has decided to change the name—while omitting the originally indispensable declared reference to Islam—into Alevite Religious Community in Austria ("*ALEVI*").[8]

5.2 Islamgesetz (the Federal Act on Islamic Religious Societies)[9]

The specific rights and obligations of the existing Islamic Alevite Religious Society in Austria are contained in Part 4 (§§16–22) of the IslamG and predominantly formulated in an equivalent form to the provisions which are provided for the Islamic Religious Society in Part 3. This applies to the following rights: the protection of the name and religious designations, the right to give opinions and make proposals to legislative and executive bodies, the protection of spiritual ministers and the professional secrecy of spiritual ministers, spiritual care to those members who are in the armed forces, who are prison inmates or patients of public healthcare and similar institutions; the guidance of their

5 Potz, Richard and Schinkele, Brigitte (fn. 2).

6 Cf. Hammer, Stefan (fn. 4).

7 For the disputed inclusion of the IAGÖ in the IslamG see Potz, Richard, and Schinkele, Brigitte, Opinion on the Draft of an Act on Islam, at http://www.parlament.gv.at/PAKT/VHG/XXV/SNME/SNME_02076/fname_371638.pdf [last accessed 20 December 2019]. See also Potz, Richard, and Schinkele, Brigitte (fn. 2).

8 §6 a) Constitution, cf. below.

9 See chapter 3.

children and young people through all traditional customs and their education in accordance with religious doctrines, the consideration of dietary laws, and regulations regarding public holidays and cemeteries.[10]

5.3 The Internal Law of the (Islamic) Alevi Religious Society in Austria

Verfassung der (Islamisch-)alevitischen Glaubensgemeinschaft in Österreich[11]

§ 1—*Name der Glaubensgemeinschaft*

(1) Die Glaubensgemeinschaft führt den Namen "Alevitische Glaubensgemeinschaft in Österreich" [...]. Die Abkürzung des Namens lautet "ALEVI".

§ 2—*Darstellung der Religionslehre*

1) Begriffserklärungen
Der Begriff „Alevi“ leitet sich vom Namen des Heiligen Ali, dem Vetter und Schwiegersohn des Propheten Mohammed ab und bedeutet demnach Anhänger Alis und derer die Ali's Lehre befolgen. Die Bezeichnung Aleviten wird als Sammelbezeichnung für die verschiedenen kulturell und geographisch bedingten Begriffe [Bektaschi/Bektaşi, Kızılbaş/Qizilbalsch/Quizilbas, Tahtacı, Sıraç, Yörük, Çepni, Abdal, (Nusayri) Arabischen Aleviten, Mevlevi, Zaidiler (Fünfer-Schia), Ismailer (Siebener-Schia), Caferi (Zwölfer-Schia) u.a.m.] verwendet. Die Glaubenslehre wird von allen vorhergenannten kulturell und geographisch bedingten Strömungen (mit wenigen Nuancen) vertreten.[12]

10 Reference is made to the relevant provisions in the respective chapters.

11 In the 2015 version of the amendment, approved by the *Kultusamt* by decision of 5 November 2015. In what follows only the principal religious assignment and the membership rules are printed.

12 This definition of Alevism includes practically all larger groups of Shiite Islam, contradicting, therefore, the self-understanding of some of these groups. At least Fiver-Shiites (Zaidis), Sevener-Shiites (Ismailis) and Twelfer-Shiites from the perspective of religious science do not count as Alevism.

§ 6—*Beginn der Mitgliedschaft*

a) Mitglieder

1) Es wird davon ausgegangen, daß jede natürliche Person, die sich zum Alevitentum bekennt und ihren Hauptwohnsitz in Österreich hat, Mitglied der ALEVI ist.[13] Die Mitgliedschaft wird im Gemeinderegister der jeweiligen Religionsgemeinde der ALEVI, in deren sachlichen u. örtlichen Wirkungskreis sich der Hauptwohnsitz des betreffenden Mitglieds befindet, erfasst. Die Erklärung der Mitgliedschaft kann durch persönliche Erklärung vor Funktionsträger [sic!] der ALEVI oder den Funktionsträgern der Religions- und Kultusgemeinde der ALEVI, oder öffentliches Bekenntnis zum Alevitentum und Abgabe des Glaubensbekenntnisses ALEVI erfolgen. Bei wirksamem Entfall der Verwendung des religiösen Oberbegriffes ISLAM für das Glaubensbekenntnis anderer islamischer Religionsgesellschaften per Gesetz oder per Verordnung kann auch auf die Verwendung des Religionsbekenntnisses ISLAM als ein Bekenntnis zur Mitgliedschaft der ALEVI als Erklärung verzichtet werden. Bleibt hingegen die Verwendung des religiösen Oberbegriff ISLAM als Glaubensbekenntnis für eine der gesetzlich anerkannten islamischen Bekenntnisgemeinschaften oder islamischen Religionsgesellschaften aufrecht, gilt die Erklärung des Religionsbegriffes ISLAM jeder natürlichen Person mit Hauptwohnsitz in Österreich auch als Erklärung zum Alevitentum und somit als Erklärung zur Mitgliedschaft zur Alevitischen Glaubensgemeinschaft in Österreich (ALEVI).[14]

Die Mitgliedschaft wird im Gemeinderegister der jeweiligen Religionsgemeinde der ALEVI, in deren sachlichen und örtlichen Wirkungskreis sich der Hauptwohnsitz des betreffenden Mitglieds befindet, erfasst.

---

13 Since only some of the Austrian Alevis agree with the concept of ALEVI, this provision is unlawful, cf. 5.1.

14 The provisions of this paragraph partly contradict Austrian law on religion and are partly unintelligible or at least misleading.

CHAPTER 6

Islamic State-Registered Religious Denominational Communities

6.1 Introduction

According to § 4 section 1 no. 2 of the BekGG, the religious doctrine of the community, which must differ from that of already existing religious denominational communities according to this federal law as well as from the doctrine of legally recognised churches and religious societies, has to be published. Since 1979 the Constitutions[1] of the IGGÖ have included at least the eight law schools, which were recognised by the summit meeting of the Organisation of the Islamic Conference in December 2005 and by the International Islamic Fiqh Academy in Jeddah,[2] including the Twelver-Shia and the Fiver-Shia (Zaidis). This in principle would exclude these eight law schools from registration as religious denominational communities and even from the establishment of associations. Nonetheless, the Shiite Religious Community claiming membership of all Muslims belonging to the Twelver-Shia and other Shiite schools (Article 1 section 6 of the Statutes, cf. below) was approved by the *Kultusamt*. Thus, the legal requirement of a different religious doctrine was de facto circumvented, since the Shiite religious community put forward specific statutes disregarding their traditional affiliation to the IGGiÖ by claiming the right to represent Shiites exclusively.[3]

6.2 Islamic-Shiite Religious Community in Austria/(Shia)—Islamisch-schiitische Glaubensgemeinschaft in Österreich (Schia)

The Islamic-Shiite Religious Community in Austria/(Shia) acquired legal personality in accordance with the BekGG on 1 March 2013.[4]

---

1 See chapter 4.3.

2 see fn. 11.

3 Meanwhile the situation has become even more confusing, since the (Islamic) Alevite religious community is claiming all Shiite schools of law and traditions as well (see chapter 5.3).

4 Decree of 28 February 2013, GZ BMUKK-12.056/0005-KA/2012.

Verfassung der Islamisch-schiitische Glaubensgemeinschaft in Österreich (Schia)[5]
Art. 1
[...]
(6) Der Islamischen-Schiitischen Glaubensgemeinschaft in Österreich gehören die Anhänger der Schia, ohne Unterschied des Geschlechts, der ethnischen Herkunft oder der Nationalität, welche in der Republik Österreich ihren Hauptwohnsitz haben, an. Die Islamische-Schiitische Glaubensgemeinschaft vertritt dabei die Rechtsschule der Imamiten (Dschafariten).
(7) Solange andere Schiiten und Rechtsschulen (Ismailiten oder Siebener-Schiiten, Zaiditen,[6] Fünfer-Schiiten, u.a.) keine eigene Glaubensgemeinschaft in Österreich gegründet haben, sind diese ebenfalls Mitglied der Islamischen-Schiitischen Glaubensgemeinschaft in Österreich, haben aber das Recht, in ihren Gebetshäusern und anderen privaten und öffentlichen Einrichtungen ihre eigene Glaubensrichtung auszuüben, wobei die ISGÖ alle religiösen Rechte und Pflichten dieser Gruppierungen übernimmt.

5 Printed in *Österreichisches Archiv für Recht und Religion*, vol. 60 (2013), pp. 148–196, in the version before the last amendment. In what follows only the principal religious assignment and the membership rules are printed.

6 Zaidis (Fiver-Shiites), as one of the eight worldwide recognised Islamic law schools (see Chapter 1, fn. 11), have since 1979 also been members of the IGGÖ (see chapter 1.2).

CHAPTER 7

Alevite State-Registered Religious Denominational Communities

7.1 Introduction

In accordance with § 4 section 1 no. 2 of the BekGG, the religious doctrine of the community has to be published and must must differ from the teaching of already existing religious confessional communities according to this federal law as well as from the teaching of legally recognised churches and religious societies.

Alevism is an independent syncretistic religion with special references to Islamic traditions. It includes, therefore, not only groups with different positions in relation to Islam, but also a wide range of different traditions.[1]

7.2 Alt-Alevitische Glaubensgemeinschaft in Österreich (AAGÖ)

With effect from 23 August 2013, the religious denominational community "Old Alevi Religious Community in Austria" acquired legal personality in accordance with § 2 section 1 of the BekGG.

In the decision of the responsible minister it is pointed out that the term "Alevis" and terms derived therefrom represent an umbrella term for different forms and groups of Alevism, comparable to Buddhism, Christianity and Islam. The choice of the name has its limits only where there is confusion or a non-existent different religious doctrine needs to be concealed.

The term "old Alevis" has no tradition within the plurality of Alevism. To what extent the term "old" should refer to an older, previous, original or even more traditional form of Alevism is a question of the self-understanding of the community and cannot be assessed in the context of an administrative procedure.

---

1 See Chapter 5.1.

…

Statuten der Alt-Alevitischen Glaubensgemeinschaft in Österreich[2]

Präambel

Das Alt-Alevitentum ist ein eigenständiger Glaube. Mit dieser Bezeichnung wird dargetan, dass sein Ursprung in den Religionen des vorislamischen bzw vorchristlichen Mittelasien und Mesopotamien liegt. Hierzu gehören der Zoroastrismus bzw Parsismus, der römisch-persische Mithras-Glaube, Ezidentum, Schabak, Haqqa, die Ahli-Haqq bzw Kakayi und der Manichäismus. Auch christliche Elemente, so vor allem aus dem ostsyrischen Christentum, wurden in das Alt-Alevitentum aufgenommen und haben dieses ebenso bereichert wie Elemente der jüdischen Kabbala. Vom schiitischen Islam und vom Sufismus hat das Alt-Alevitentum schließlich seine letzte Prägung und auch den Namen übernommen, ohne dass es damit zu einer islamischen Glaubensrichtung wurde. Ein wichtiger Aspekt der alt-alevitischen Religion ist auch der Schamanismus, der in den Ritualen bis heute eine Rolle spielt. Auf vielerlei Art und Weise kann man sehen, dass diese Religionsgemeinschaften, die man heutzutage in Kurdistan antrifft, sich über verschiedene Elemente miteinander verbunden, neue Glaubensrichtungen begründet haben und es verschiedene grundlegende Gemeinsamkeiten unter diesen Religionen gibt.

…

Art. 4—*Erwerb der Mitgliedschaft*

(1) Personen, die sich zum alt-alevitischen Glauben bekennen und ihren Hauptwohnsitz in Österreich haben, sind Mitglieder der AAGG. Die Mitgliedschaft wird in das Mitgliederregister der Glaubensgemeinschaft eingetragen Der Nachweis der Mitgliedschaft erfolgt durch einen schriftlichen Auszug aus diesem Register.

(2) Kinder erwerben die Mitgliedschaft durch die alt-alevitische Aufnahmezeremonie. Am 3. Tag nach der Geburt des Kindes wird ein spezielles Brot gebacken ("Lokma"). Das Kind wird neben dem Brot von einer beliebigen Person drei Mal hochgehoben. Dabei wird drei Mal der Name des Kindes ausgesprochen ("Dein Name ist …"). Am 40. Tage nach der Geburt des Kindes wird nach dem gründlichen Waschen des Kindes ein Sieb, in dem sich ein Ring eines Elternteiles befindet, über den Kopf des Kindes gehalten, wodurch 40 Löffel Wasser über den Kopf des Kindes geschüttet

2 Printed in *Österreichisches Archiv für Recht und Religion*, vol. 60 (2013), pp. 92–101. In what follows only the principal religious assignment and the membership rules are printed.

werden. Mit jedem Löffel Wasser wird das Kind an die 40 Pforten erinnert. (3) Daneben gibt es auch die Möglichkeit durch Erlernen der alevitischen Traditionen und Rituale und durch Teilnahme an den "Cems" nach Verstreichen einer Probefrist von einem Jahr in die alevitische Glaubensgemeinschaft aufgenommen zu werden. Über die Aufnahme von Mitgliedern entscheidet der Vorstand endgültig.

CHAPTER 8

Muslims in Integration Law

Integration law is a legal matter of increasing importance. In 2017 a bundle of laws was enacted which was directly relevant for integration.[1] It includes two new laws: the Act on Integration (*Bundesgesetz zur Integration rechtmäßig in Österreich aufhältiger Personen ohne österreichische Staatsbürgerschaft*—IntG) and the Anti-Face-Covering Act (*Bundesgesetz über das Verbot der Verhüllung des Gesichts in der Öffentlichkeit*—AGesVG) as well as the amendment of five laws, the Act on Asylum 2005 (Asylgesetz—AsylG), the Act on Settlement and Residence 2005 (*Bundesgesetz über die Niederlassung und den Aufenthalt in Österreich*—NAG), the Act on Aliens' Police 2005 (*Fremdenpolizeigesetz*—FPG), the Act on Citizenship 1985 (*Staatsbürgerschaftsgesetz*—StbG) and the Road Traffic Regulations 1960 (*Straßenverkehrsordnung*—StVO).

Although all these provisions do not explicitly refer to Islam or Muslims, they include in many cases indirect references to Muslims, who are assumed to be less willing to accept fundamental European values. In this sense, the Explanatory Notes to the IntG emphasise the aim of the law: "[s]uccessful integration requires that immigrants actively participate in this process, take advantage of the integration measures offered, in particular learning the German language, and knowing and respecting the basic values of a European democratic state."[2]

The Anti-Face-Covering Act, part of the legislation of 2017, is justified by the fact that it serves to promote integration by strengthening participation in society and ensuring peaceful coexistence in Austria. Integration is to be seen as a process for society as a whole, the success of which depends on the participation of all people living in Austria and is based on personal interaction (§ 1).

The reason for the insertion of Section 83 (3) into the Road Traffic Regulation was Salafist Koran distribution campaigns in Viennese shopping streets. According to the explanatory notes to the bill, it "is intended to prevent distri-

1 Integration law is a cross-sectional matter even more than law on religion. This is related to the fact that the Federal Constitution does not contain a regulation of core competence for "integration", so that different competence provisions must be used for legal regulations relevant for integration. See Gartner-Müller, Barbara, "Integration, Recht und Religion", in *Österreichisches Archiv für Recht und Religion*, vol. 64 (2017), pp. 73–96.

2 NR GP XXV, RV 1586: https://www.parlament.gv.at/PAKT/VHG/XXV/I/I_01586/fname_624803.pdf, p. 1 [last accessed 25 March 2020].

bution campaigns whose purpose is directed against public order or security, such as for the purpose of disseminating radical ideas."[3]

Provisions relevant to integration as a cross-sectional matter can be found in various fields. They are partially cited in the appropriate context, as for instance in Educational Law,[4] Employment Law,[5] Dress Law[6] and Criminal Law.[7]

Bundesgesetz zur Integration rechtmäßig in Österreich aufhältiger Personen ohne österreichische Staatsbürgerschaft (Integrationsgesetz—IntG) BGBl. I Nr. 68/2017 as amended BGBl. I Nr. 41/2019

1. Teil—*Allgemeine Bestimmungen*

§ 1—*Ziel*

(1) Das Ziel dieses Bundesgesetzes besteht in der raschen Integration rechtmäßig in Österreich aufhältiger Personen in die österreichische Gesellschaft durch das systematische Anbieten von Integrationsmaßnahmen (Integrationsförderung) sowie durch die Verpflichtung, aktiv am Integrationsprozess mitzuwirken (Integrationspflicht).
(2) Österreichs liberales und demokratisches Staatswesen beruht auf Werten und Prinzipien, die nicht zur Disposition stehen. Diese identitätsbildende Prägung der Republik Österreich und ihrer Rechtsordnung ist zu respektieren. Sie bildet die Grundlage für das friedliche Zusammenleben von Menschen unterschiedlicher Herkunft und damit für den Zusammenhalt der Gesellschaft in Österreich. Dies zu wahren ist ebenfalls Ziel dieses Bundesgesetzes.

§ 2—*Integrationsbegriff*

(1) Integration ist ein gesamtgesellschaftlicher Prozess, dessen Gelingen von der Mitwirkung aller in Österreich lebenden Menschen abhängt und auf persönlicher Interaktion beruht. Integration erfordert insbesondere,

3 NR GP XXV, RV 1586: https://www.parlament.gv.at/PAKT/VHG/XXV/I/I_01586/fname_624803.pdf, pp. 13–14 [last accessed 25 March 2020].
4 Cf. chapters 12 and 13.
5 The "Act concerning the Employment of Foreigners within the Federal Territory" (Ausländerbeschäftigungsgesetz) is included in this chapter. For further laws regarding employment with relevance for integration see chapter 15.5.
6 Cf. chapter 17.
7 Cf. chapter 19.

dass die Zugewanderten aktiv an diesem Prozess mitwirken, die angebotenen Integrationsmaßnahmen wahrnehmen und die Grundwerte eines europäischen demokratischen Staates anerkennen und respektieren. Auch alle staatlichen Institutionen auf Bundes-, Landes- und Gemeindeebene haben im Rahmen ihrer Zuständigkeiten ihren Beitrag zu einem erfolgreichen Integrationsprozess durch das systematische Anbieten von Integrationsmaßnahmen zu leisten. Integration als gesamtgesellschaftlicher Prozess erfordert ein aufeinander abgestimmtes Vorgehen der unterschiedlichen staatlichen und zivilgesellschaftlichen Akteure und setzt einen aktiven Beitrag jeder einzelnen Person in Österreich im Rahmen ihrer eigenen Möglichkeiten voraus.
(2) Integrationsmaßnahmen sollen zur Teilhabe am gesellschaftlichen, wirtschaftlichen und kulturellen Leben in Österreich befähigen. Zentral sind dabei die Teilhabe durch Erwerbsarbeit, der Zugang zu und die Annahme von Bildungsangeboten, die Gleichstellung der Geschlechter und das rasche Erreichen der Selbsterhaltungsfähigkeit. Der Erhalt der österreichischen Staatsbürgerschaft soll den Endpunkt eines umfassenden Integrationsprozesses darstellen.

§ 3—*Geltungsbereich*

Dieses Bundesgesetz regelt in den Bereichen Sprachförderung und Orientierung die Integration folgender rechtmäßig in Österreich aufhältiger Personen, die nicht über die österreichische Staatsbürgerschaft verfügen:
1. Asylberechtigte gemäß § 2 Abs. 1 Z 15 Asylgesetz 2005 (AsylG 2005), BGBl. I Nr. 100/2005,
2. subsidiär Schutzberechtigte gemäß § 2 Abs. 1 Z 16 AsylG 2005,
3. Drittstaatsangehörige gemäß § 2 Abs. 1 Z 6 Niederlassungs- und Aufenthaltsgesetz (NAG), BGBl. I Nr. 100/2005, die rechtmäßig niedergelassen sind (§ 2 Abs. 2 NAG).

Bundesgesetz über das Verbot der Verhüllung des Gesichts in der Öffentlichkeit (Anti-Gesichtsverhüllungsgesetz—AGesVG)
BGBl. I Nr. 68/2017

§ 1—*Ziel*

Ziele dieses Bundesgesetzes sind die Förderung von Integration durch die Stärkung der Teilhabe an der Gesellschaft und die Sicherung des friedlichen Zusammenlebens in Österreich. Integration ist ein gesamtgesellschaftlicher Prozess, dessen Gelingen von der Mitwirkung aller in Österreich lebenden Menschen abhängt und auf persönlicher Interaktion beruht.

§ 2—*Verhüllungsverbot*

(1) Wer an öffentlichen Orten oder in öffentlichen Gebäuden seine Gesichtszüge durch Kleidung oder andere Gegenstände in einer Weise verhüllt oder verbirgt, dass sie nicht mehr erkennbar sind, begeht eine Verwaltungsübertretung und ist mit einer Geldstrafe bis zu 150 Euro zu bestrafen. Die Verwaltungsübertretung kann durch Organstrafverfügung gemäß § 50 VStG in der Höhe von bis zu 150 Euro geahndet werden. Öffentliche Orte oder öffentliche Gebäude sind Orte, die von einem nicht von vornherein beschränkten Personenkreis ständig oder zu bestimmten Zeiten betreten werden können, einschließlich der nicht ortsfesten Einrichtungen des öffentlichen und privaten Bus-, Schienen-, Flug- und Schiffsverkehrs.
(2) Ein Verstoß gegen das Verhüllungsverbot gemäß Abs. 1 liegt nicht vor, wenn die Verhüllung oder Verbergung der Gesichtszüge durch Bundes- oder Landesgesetz vorgesehen ist, im Rahmen künstlerischer, kultureller oder traditioneller Veranstaltungen oder im Rahmen der Sportausübung erfolgt oder gesundheitliche oder berufliche Gründe hat.

§ 3—*Zuständigkeit*

Die Durchführung des Verwaltungsstrafverfahrens wegen eines Verstoßes gegen § 2 obliegt den Bezirksverwaltungsbehörden, im Gebiet einer Gemeinde, für das die Landespolizeidirektion zugleich Sicherheitsbehörde erster Instanz ist, dieser. § 86 Abs. 2 Sicherheitspolizeigesetz (SPG), BGBl. Nr. 566/1991, gilt sinngemäß.

Bundesgesetz über die Niederlassung und den Aufenthalt in Österreich (Niederlassungs- und Aufenthaltsgesetz—NAG)
BGBl. I Nr. 100/2005 as amended BGBl. I Nr. 104/2019

…

§ 2

(1) Im Sinne dieses Bundesgesetzes ist
[...]
9. Familienangehöriger: wer Ehegatte oder minderjähriges lediges Kind, einschließlich Adoptiv- oder Stiefkind, ist (Kernfamilie); dies gilt weiters auch für eingetragene Partner; Ehegatten und eingetragene Partner müssen das 21. Lebensjahr zum Zeitpunkt der Antragstellung bereits vollendet haben; lebt im Fall einer Mehrfachehe[8] bereits ein Ehegatte gemeinsam mit dem Zusammenführenden im Bundesgebiet, so sind die weiteren Ehegatten keine anspruchsberechtigten Familienangehörigen zur Erlangung eines Aufenthaltstitels;
...

Bundesgesetz vom 20. März 1975, mit dem die Beschäftigung von Ausländern geregelt wird (Ausländerbeschäftigungsgesetz—AuslBG)
BGBl. Nr. 218/1975 as amended BGBl. I Nr. 104/2019

Abschnitt I—*Allgemeine Bestimmungen*

§ 1—*Geltungsbereich*

(1) Dieses Bundesgesetz regelt die Beschäftigung von Ausländern (§ 2) im Bundesgebiet.
(2) Die Bestimmungen dieses Bundesgesetzes sind nicht anzuwenden auf
...
d) Ausländer hinsichtlich ihrer seelsorgerischen Tätigkeiten im Rahmen von gesetzlich anerkannten Kirchen und Religionsgesellschaften;

Bundesgesetz über die österreichische Staatsbürgerschaft (Staatsbürgerschaftsgesetz—StbG)
BGBl. Nr. 311/1985 as amended BGBl. I Nr. 96/2019

...

8 For the treatment of polygamy in Austrian law see chapter 18.1.

§ 11

Bei Entscheidungen nach diesem Bundesgesetz ist das Gesamtverhalten des Fremden im Hinblick auf das allgemeine Wohl, die öffentlichen Interessen und das Ausmaß seiner Integration zu berücksichtigen. Zu dieser zählt insbesondere die Orientierung des Fremden am gesellschaftlichen, wirtschaftlichen und kulturellen Leben in Österreich sowie das Bekenntnis zu den Grundwerten eines europäischen demokratischen Staates und seiner Gesellschaft.

...

Case Law

Case 1: §§ 11 ff. of the StbG require the extent of integration to be considered as a whole. The alleged behaviour of the first applicant in refusing to shake hands cannot be used as the sole indicator for the degree of personal integration. A long lawful stay and the resulting personal anchorage in Austria (the applicant's family lives with him in Austria, the children attend school here), as well as his employment as an teacher of religious education since 1999, speak for a sufficient degree of integration: VwGH 15. 3. 2010, 2008/01/0552.

Case 2: Monogamy and the prohibition of multiple marriages (bigamy) are two of the indispensable basic values that shape the Austrian legal system.[9] The justification that he entered into the second marriage "only" for religious reasons proves that it can be assumed that the applicant for the award of Austrian citizenship in accordance with § 11 of the StbG is not committed to the basic values of a European democratic state and its society: VwGH 6. 9. 2018, Ra 2018/18/0094; 11. 10. 2019, Ra 2019/01/0373.

Straßenverkehrsordnung 1960 (StVO 1960)
BGBl. Nr. 159/1960 as amended BGBl. I Nr. 113/2019
...
Benützung von Straßen zu verkehrsfremden Zwecken

Bewilligungspflicht

9 Cf. the case law on § 6 IPRG, chapter 18.3.

§ 82

(1) Für die Benützung von Straßen einschließlich des darüber befindlichen, für die Sicherheit des Straßenverkehrs in Betracht kommenden Luftraumes zu anderen Zwecken als zu solchen des Straßenverkehrs, z. B. zu gewerblichen Tätigkeiten und zur Werbung, ist unbeschadet sonstiger Rechtsvorschriften eine Bewilligung nach diesem Bundesgesetz erforderlich. Das gleiche gilt für Tätigkeiten, die geeignet sind, Menschenansammlungen auf der Straße herbeizuführen oder die Aufmerksamkeit der Lenker von Fahrzeugen zu beeinträchtigen.
...

§ 83
[...]
(3) Ist aufgrund bestimmter Tatsachen anzunehmen, dass der Zweck des Vorhabens (§ 82 Abs. 1) gegen die öffentliche Ordnung im Sinne des § 81 SPG oder öffentliche Sicherheit verstößt, so sind davon die Sicherheitsbehörden in Kenntnis zu setzen. Eine Bewilligung nach § 82 Abs. 1 ist nicht zu erteilen, wenn die jeweilige Landespolizeidirektion in der Stellungnahme erklärt hat, dass die Durchführung des Vorhabens (§ 82 Abs. 1) eine Gefährdung der öffentlichen Ordnung oder Sicherheit darstellen würde. Die Stellungnahme ist ohne unnötigen Aufschub, möglichst innerhalb von 10 Werktagen zu übermitteln.

CHAPTER 9

The Financing of Islamic Religious Societies

In Austria there is no general state funding for churches and religious societies.[1] State payments to religious communities as such exist only on the basis of an indemnity for financial losses caused during the Nazi occupation, which is not relevant to the Islamic community.

However, state financing is permitted in the case where welfare services delivered by religious institutions are reimbursed from public funds, direct funding is provided in the school sector and indirect through tax exemptions.

The special Acts for recognised churches and religious societies regularly contain regulations regarding membership contributions which can be enforced before state courts and administrative authorities.

9.1 Cultus Contributions

According to the unanimous opinion of the high courts the independent administration of property constitutes an "internal matter" with regard to churches and religious societies.[2]

§ 23 section 1 of the IslamG 2015 provides that the "cultus contribution regulation" (*Kultusumlagenordnung*) of an Islamic Religious Society requires the approval of the *Kultusamt*.

According to § 4 of the Statute of the IGGÖ, every member of the Islamic Religious Society of Austria has to pay an annual fee of a maximum of EUR 60. The possibility of administrative enforcement is provided for by law, but the Islamic Religious Society does not use this instrument at the present time.

According to § 6 section 3 of the Statute of the (I)AGÖ, the amount of the membership fees and the modalities of collection are determined by the Federal Assembly.

1 As in East European countries, the sources of revenue for religious communities are an amalgamation of membership contributions, voluntary grants, such as donations, inheritances, charity benefit contributions, income from estates and capital assets, and profits from businesses and enterprises.

2 Constitutional Court, VfSlg 3816/1960; Supreme Administrative Court, VwGH 3. 10. 1967, 1433/64; Supreme Court, OGH 14. 5. 1958, 2Ob143/58; Supreme Court, OGH 27. 8. 1952, 3Ob509/52.

9.2 Foreign Financing of Normal Activities

§ 6 section 2 of the IslamG explicitly stipulates for Islamic Religious Societies that the financial means for normal activities aimed at satisfying the religious needs of their members must be obtained by the Religious Society, its worship communities or its members from within the country. In the Explanatory Notes to the bill[3] it is stated—for the first time and not without challenge—that the prohibition of core funding from abroad was implicitly included even in § 5 of the AnerkennungsG 1874.[4]

Case Law

Case 1: The prohibition of the financing of the ordinary activities of Islamic religious societies by foreign states and their institutions does not infringe Article 9 ECHR. In § 6 section 2, the principle of self-supporting, laid down in § 4 section 1 of the IslamG as well as in § 5 and § 1 section 2 of the AnerkennungsG,[5] was concretised in specifically for the Islamic religious societies and cultus communities. Although the raising and use of financial resources is in principle part of the "internal affairs" within the meaning of Article 15 of the StGG, the prohibition of funding through foreign finance is to ensure the autonomy, and thus the free exercise of religion on the part of the members and the independent administration of the "internal affairs" of the Islamic religious societies or communities against the influence of other states and their institutions—in the concrete case: the Presidium for Religious Affairs of the Republic of Turkey (*Diyanet İşleri Başkanlığı*). The Constitutional Court admittedly carried out a teleological reduction of the legal provision in so far as it stressed that the provision in conformity with the constitution has to be applied to contributions from other states and their institutions and not to foreign private funding, if they do not have a comparable autonomy-restricting effect: VfGH 13th, 2019, E3830/2018 et alia.

3 NR GP XXV, RV 446: https://www.parlament.gv.at/PAKT/VHG/XXV/I/I_00446/fname_377359.pdf, pp. 4–5 [last accessed 20 March 2020].

4 Cf. fn. 17.

5 Cf. fn. 17.

9.3 Tax Law

The provisions of tax law which are relevant to religious societies are, on the one hand, based on the consequences in revenue law resulting from the public-law status of legally recognised churches and religious societies, hence mainly concerned with corporate income tax liability and value added tax liability. On the other hand, Austrian tax law provides for benefits, i.e. reductions or exemptions for corporations which pursue "ecclesiastical aims" in addition to those with public utility or charitable purposes. According to § 38 section 1 of the Federal Revenue Act 1961 (*Bundesabgabenordnung*, BAO),[6] "ecclesiastical aims" are those aims which promote legally recognised churches and religious societies. § 38 section 2 contains a representative list of such "ecclesiastical purposes" which must be met if a tax law, in connection with preferential treatment of private law corporations, associations and assets, refers *inter alia* to religious purposes:

> Ecclesiastical purposes include in particular the establishment, maintenance and decoration of buildings of worship and parish houses, the holding of religious services, prayers and other religious or pastoral events, the training of religious ministers, religious education classes, funerals and religious commemoration of the dead, furthermore, the administration of church property, remuneration of the clergy and church employees, provision for their old age and invalidity, care of their widows and orphans including the establishment and maintenance of special facilities for this group (§ 38 section 2 of the BAO).

To obtain these benefits, the statutes of the corporations concerned must expressly and precisely describe the exclusive and immediate activities involved in such "ecclesiastical purposes."

Furthermore, in accordance with § 2 no. 5 and 6 of the Landtax Act,[7] for certain religious uses of land (religious services, pastoral care or religious instruction, administrative purposes, homes for the elderly) no land tax is payable.

Contributions to legally recognised churches and religious societies are tax deductable as special payments up to an annual amount of EUR 400.

---

6 BGBl. Nr. 194/1961 as amended BGBl. I Nr. 2/2020.

7 *Grundsteuergesetz*, BGBl. Nr. 149/1955 as amended BGBl. I Nr. 104/2019.

9.4 Indirect Financing of Religious Communities

Additional state subsidies are granted for specific religious activities in the field of education (Religious Instruction,[8] Theological Studies,[9] denominational Private Schools)[10] and for chaplaincies in the armed forces.

Church activities in the field of social assistance and health care, education and culture, though hardly ascertainable, represent a significant instrument for legitimating their status. Primary statistical data for this non-profit sector are not available.

8 See chapter 12.

9 See chapter 13.

10 See chapter 12.6.

CHAPTER 10

Mosques and Prayer Rooms

Freedom of religion and belief guarantees full freedom for the undisturbed exercise of religious and non-religious behaviours, thus encompassing the construction of buildings or places of worship. A substantive approach in the interpretation of fundamental rights as well as state neutrality in religious matters requires the state to consider the religious interests and needs of the faithful when preparing plans for land use.

Provisions regarding urban and regional planning as well as building regulations fall within the competence of the *Bundesländer* (federal states). Consequently, in the context of the systematic and future-oriented structuring of the national territory, the Regional Planning Acts of the *Bundesländer* must be fully sensitive to the cultural requirements and needs of the population. The cultural environment, as one of the foundations of the development of a comprehensive personality, also includes the religious dimension and, consequently, religious buildings, as a requirement for the practice of worship and related activities, according to the religious concept in question. After having assessed the appropriate space requirements of each religious community irrespective of their legal status, municipal development planners must reserve areas to include facilities for pastoral care, amongst other things.

Urban and regional planning programmes must be sent to the legally recognised churches and religious societies, or at least to the Catholic Church and the Protestant Church, for their opinions.

Similarly, in compliance with the aforementioned requirements, building regulation laws must guarantee the undisturbed practice of religion with regard to buildings intended for worship, such as churches, mosques, synagogues and other buildings of this kind. Consequently, the general rules concerning construction height do not regularly apply to such buildings as long as the urban image and landscape are not impaired. However, structural engineering requirements concerning general criteria such as safety, strength of buildings, fire protection, environmental protection or the like are relevant also for religious buildings.

There are some seemingly neutral building regulation laws at the level of the *Landes*-legislature which are politically intended massively to complicate the building of mosques.[1]

1 Although these laws must, in fact, be considered unconstitutional, there has, hitherto, been no complaint giving an opportunity to examine their constitutionality.

In Carinthia, on the occasion of an application for building permission for a mosque, the Building Regulation Act (*Kärtner Bauordnung*, Ktn-BauO 1996)[2] and the Act on Townscape Care (*Kärtner Ortsbildpflegegesetz*, Ktn-OrtsbildpflG 1990)[3] were amended in 2009. The core content of the revised version was the establishment of a Special Commission for townscape care with the task of "assess[ing] … what is customary in the locality or local standards." The legislative process was accompanied by the openly declared political intention to complicate the construction of mosques in particular.[4]

In 2008, a special procedure for townscape care was introduced in Vorarlberg.[5] Since then, the Government of the *Land* Vorarlberg has been entitled to determine by ordinance which construction projects affect the interests of townscape or landscape protection due to type, size and shape. Furthermore, in the Vorarlberg Act on Land-Use Planning the concept of "locations for large audiences" was established (§ 16b).[6] Under this provision, the municipal council can determine by ordinance that locations for large audiences need special treatment in the zoning plan. An appropriate location must be designed for at least 150 people; examples mentioned are cinema centres, discotheques, sports facilities and buildings for worship. In the legislative process it was emphasised here too that mosques were the focus of attention.

With regard to buildings for worship, the question of noise emissions also arises. In these cases one has to consider the protection of religious practice and observances on the one hand, and the limitations of religious manifestations in order to protect legitimate conflicting interests on the other. In practice the problems were originally related to the ringing of church bells. The same is true with regard to the muezzin's call to prayer which is, in principle, allowed and can, after all, also be transmitted via loudspeaker. However, an appropriate level of noise pollution must not be exceeded. Case by case, a fair balance

---

2 LGBl. Nr. 62/1996 as amended LGBl. Nr. 16/2009.

3 LGBl. Nr. 32/1990 as amended LGBl. 16/2009.

4 See Heine, Susanne, Lohlker, Rüdiger, and Potz, Richard, *Islam in Österreich* (Innsbruck & Vienna: Tyrolia-Verlag, 2012), pp. 127 ff.; Hafez, Farid, and Potz, Richard, "Moscheebau- und Minarettverbote in Österreich", in Bunzl, John, and Hafez, Farid (eds.), *Islamophobie in Österreich* (Innsbruck et al.: Studienverlag, 2009), pp. 143–155; Wieshaider, Wolfgang, "Profane Regeln für sakrale Bauten. Religionsrechtliche Aspekte des Raumordnungs- und Baurechts," in *Baurechtliche Blätter*, vol. 6 (2003), pp. 138 ff.; Fürlinger, Ernst, *Moscheebaukonflikte in Österreich. Nationale Politik des religiösen Raums im globalen Zeitalter* (Vienna: University Press, 2013).

5 Vorarlberg Building Regulation Act (*Vorarlberger Baugesetz*, Vlbg-BauG 2001), LGBl. Nr. 52/2001 as amended LGBl. Nr. 34/2008.

6 Vorarlberg Act on Land-Use Planning (*Vorarlberger Raumplanungsgesetz*, Vlbg-RaumplG 1996), LGBl. Nr. 39/1996 as amended LGBl. 35/2008.

must be struck between religious interests and the needs of neighbours and the general surroundings.

Under public law, the various Security Laws of the *Bundesländer* contain provisions on "undue emission of disturbing noise" as an administrative offence.[7] Usually, conflicts arising can be settled by mutual agreement.

On the level of private law, § 364 of the Austrian Civil Law Code (ABGB) stipulates that private owners of real property must obey limitations emanating from the laws which serve the preservation and promotion of the common good. Accordingly, impacts by emissions are forbidden if they exceed the usual customary standards. As far as the muezzin's call is concerned, local standards are to be interpreted with respect to the fundamental guarantee of religious freedom as well as changed demographic conditions.

7 Cf. for instance Styrian Security Act (*Steiermärkisches Landes-Sicherheitsgesetz*, St-LSiG), LGBl. Nr. 88/2005 as amended LGBl. Nr. 147/2013; Viennese Security Act (*Wiener Landes-Sicherheitsgesetz*, Wr-LSiG), LGBl. Nr. 51/1993 as amended LGBl. Nr. 71/2018.

CHAPTER 11

Islamic Funerals and Graveyards

11.1 State Regulations

In accordance with Article 10 Para. 1 No. 12 in conjunction with Article 15 of the B-VG, the competence for dealing with corpses, funeral services and graveyards lies with the federal states. According to Article 118 para. 2 and para. 3 No. 7 of the B-VG, enforcement of the laws is the duty of the municipalities. Hereby the provisions of §§ 15 and 22 IslamG[1] must be observed, according to which cemeteries and cemetery sections are conceived of as permanent. Their dissolution or closure or the exhumation of individual graves is prohibited. Exceptions require the approval of the competent religious authority. Burials in Islamic cemeteries and cemetery sections may be carried out only with the approval of the competent religious authority.

11.2 Islamic Funeral Provisions

There are principal restrictions with regard to those Islamic regulations that contradict the usual funeral regulations in Austria—burial within 24 hours after death and burial in a shroud instead of a coffin.

11.3 Islamic Graveyards

There are two Islamic cemeteries, where some of the Islamic provisions are taken into account.

The Vienna Islamic Cemetery, opened on 3 October 2008, is a denominational facility sponsored by the IGGÖ. Funerals are carried out by the undertaker of the Municipality of Vienna ("Bestattung Wien") in cooperation with the IGGÖ. A package is offered that contains the complete organisation and processing of a funeral according to the Islamic rites: the necessary documents are provided, the date for the ritual washing is fixed, the farewell in the prayer hall and the funeral in the Islamic cemetery are organised.[2]

1 See chapter 3.

2 https://www.derislam.at/einrichtungen/friedhof/ (last accessed on 1 July 2020).

On 2 June 2012 the second separate cemetery for Muslims in Austria was opened in Altach/Vorarlberg. The Islamic Cemetery Altach is a municipal facility managed by the municipality of Altach, but is open to Muslims from all over Vorarlberg.[3]

Bestattungsanlagenordnung: Islamischer Friedhof in Wien 23[4]
1. Präambel
Der islamische Friedhof (in der Folge „IFH“ abgekürzt) ist ein konfessioneller Friedhof für Muslime. Der Rechtsträger des Friedhofes ist die islamische Glaubensgemeinschaft in Österreich (in der Folge „IGGÖ abgekürzt). Ihr obliegt die Verwaltung des IFH.
Der Islam betrachtet alle Lebewesen und insbesondere Menschen als ehrwürdig. Die Existenz dieser hört mit dem Tod nicht auf. Der menschliche Körper muss daher mit allem Respekt und Achtung behandelt werden. Zu den Respekt- und Hygienehandlungen zählen unter anderem ein schnelles Begräbnis und die rituelle Waschung davor.
Soweit in dieser Bestattungsanlagenordnung personenbezogene Bezeichnungen nur in männlicher Form angeführt sind, beziehen sie sich auf Frauen und Männer in gleicher Weise.

2. ALLGEMEINE BESTIMMUNGEN
2.1 Geltungsbereich
(1) Diese Bestattungsanlagenordnung (im Sinne des § 32 Abs. 2 Wiener Leichen- und Bestattungsgesetz) gilt ab Eröffnung des IFH als Hausordnung und als generelle Grundlage einer privatrechtlichen Vereinbarung zwischen der islamischen Religionsgemeinschaft und den Benützungsberechtigten an den Grabstellen.
(2) Die Bestimmungen des Wiener Leichen- und Bestattungsgesetzes sind zu beachten.

…

3 https://www.derislam.at/einrichtungen/friedhof/ (last accessed on 1 July 2020).
4 Made available by the IGGÖ.

CHAPTER 12

Education and Schooling

12.1 Constitutional Guarantees

The main competences regarding schools lie with the *Bund*,[1] whereby some subjects are deemed to be of paramount significance and, therefore, subject to the requirement of a two-thirds majority of a quorum of at least 50 per cent of the Members of Parliament (Article 14 section 10). Amongst these subjects are "affairs concerning state-church-relations" including religious school instruction and matters of denominational private schools (*konfessionelle Privatschulen*).

Pursuant to Article 17 section 2 of the StGG, the establishment and management of private schools and other educational institutions is guaranteed provided their legal qualifications can be assured. As far as the fundamental right of parents to educate their children privately at home without attending school is concerned (Article 17 section 3 StGG), the requirements of compulsory schooling are considered to be met pursuant to § 11 Act on Compulsory Schooling (*Schulpflichtgesetz*, SchPflG)[2] only if home education has the same quality as that of public schools or private schools with public status, though any state influence on the structure of home instruction is excluded. The success of home schooling has to be validated by the taking of an examination at an appropriate public school every year.[3]

According to Article 14 section 5a of the Federal Constitution (*Bundesverfassungsgesetz*, B-VG), it is the aim of Austrian schooling to contribute to the development of the aptitudes of young people—amongst other things—regarding religious values by appropriate instruction.

Bundes-Verfassungsgesetz (B-VG) 1920
BGBl. Nr. 1/1930 as amended BGBl. I Nr. 47/2019

1 These general constitutional provisions regarding schools are not printed here.

2 BGBl. Nr. 76/1985 as amended BGBl. I Nr. 86/2019.

3 Cf. Hammer, Stefan, and Franck, Thomas, "Religion in Public Education—Report on Austria," in European Consortium of Church & State Research (ed.), *Religion in Public Education* (Trier: University of Trier, 2011), pp. 61 ff.

Art. 14

...

(5a) Demokratie, Humanität, Solidarität, Friede und Gerechtigkeit sowie Offenheit und Toleranz gegenüber den Menschen sind Grundwerte der Schule, auf deren Grundlage sie der gesamten Bevölkerung, unabhängig von Herkunft, sozialer Lage und finanziellem Hintergrund, unter steter Sicherung und Weiterentwicklung bestmöglicher Qualität ein höchstmögliches Bildungsniveau sichert. Im partnerschaftlichen Zusammenwirken von Schülern, Eltern und Lehrern ist Kindern und Jugendlichen die bestmögliche geistige, seelische und körperliche Entwicklung zu ermöglichen, damit sie zu gesunden, selbstbewussten, glücklichen, leistungsorientierten, pflichttreuen, musischen und kreativen Menschen werden, die befähigt sind, an den sozialen, religiösen und moralischen Werten orientiert Verantwortung für sich selbst, Mitmenschen, Umwelt und nachfolgende Generationen zu übernehmen. Jeder Jugendliche soll seiner Entwicklung und seinem Bildungsweg entsprechend zu selbständigem Urteil und sozialem Verständnis geführt werden, dem politischen, religiösen und weltanschaulichen Denken anderer aufgeschlossen sein sowie befähigt werden, am Kultur- und Wirtschaftsleben Österreichs, Europas und der Welt teilzunehmen und in Freiheits- und Friedensliebe an den gemeinsamen Aufgaben der Menschheit mitzuwirken.

12.2 Religious Education

The Act on the Religious Upbringing of Children of 1985[4] (*Bundesgesetz über die religiöse Kindererziehung*, RelKErzG) provides a detailed structure for achieving religious maturity. Parents are able freely to decide on the religious upbringing of a child insofar as they have the right of parental care and responsibility for raising the child. This agreement can be revoked at any time and is dissolved by the death of one of the spouses (§1 of the RelKErzG). After the age of 14, the child is free to decide about its religious confession. After it reaches the age of 12, the child's religious confession may not be changed against its will (§5 of the RelKErzG).

According to §11 section 4 and §18 section 4 of the IslamG 2015,[5] religious societies and their members are entitled to guide their children and young

4 Re-enactment of the (German) Act on the Religious Upbringing of Children 1921/1939, BGBl. Nr. 155/1985.

5 See chapter 3.

people through all traditional customs and to educate them according to their religious commandments. The explanatory notes to these provisions explicitly point out that male circumcision is covered by them.[6]

12.3 Religion and Schooling—General Introduction

The Constitutional basis for the field of religion and school is to be found in Articles 15 and 17 of the StGG 1867.[7] In accordance with these constitutional provisions, on 25 May 1868 the law "whereby basic provisions on the relationship of the school to the church are enacted" was passed (*Schule-Kirche-Gesetz*[8]). Although this law is formally still in force, its content has been superceded by the Act on Religious Education at School (*Bundesgesetz betreffend den Religionsunterricht in der Schule*, ReligionsunterrichtsG)[9] and the Private School Act (*Bundesgesetz über das Privatschulwesen*, PrivatschulG).[10]

12.4 School Time Regulations

According to § 13 sections 1 and 2 of the Act on Teaching-time at Schools (*Schulzeitgesetz*, SchZG),[11] Muslim and Alevite pupils do not have to attend school on some high holidays.[12] The dates will be announced by the IGGÖ, the AGÖ and by the Islamic-Shiite Religious Community, and decrees of the Minister of Education[13] recommend giving permission to stay away from school lessons on those days in accordance with § 9 section 6 of the Act on Compulsory Schooling (*Schulpflichtgesetz*) 1985.[14]

6 Cf. chapter 17.2.
7 See chapter2.1.
8 RGBl. Nr. 48/1868.
9 See below.
10 See below.
11 BGBl. Nr. 77/1985 as amended BGBl. I Nr. 49/2019.
12 See below.
13 Actually, BMBWF-21.001/0007-II/4/2019, BMB-21.001/0002-Präs.12/2017, BMB-21.001/0001-Präs.12/2017.
14 BGBl. Nr. 76/1985 as amended BGBl. I Nr. 23/2020.

12.5 Religious Instruction

12.5.1 *General Remarks*

Religious instruction is guaranteed by Article 17 section 4 of the StGG[15] which provides that churches or religious societies are responsible for religious instruction in schools.[16] Viewed systematically, religious instruction must be seen in relation to the fundamental right to religious freedom and the guarantees in Article 2 of Additional Protocol 1 to the ECHR, with regard to pupils as well as parents, on the one hand, and the organisational religious freedom of religious communities on the other. However, for historical reasons, the right to give religious instruction in schools is restricted to legally recognised churches and religious societies.

Currently, religious instruction is governed by the Act on Religious Education at School of 1949 (RelUG). According to § 1 of the RelUG, all pupils who are members of a legally recognised church or religious society must take religious instruction in their denomination as a compulsory subject in primary and secondary schools, colleges of education, academies for social work, teacher training colleges, agricultural colleges and colleges of forestry. In other schools religious instruction is an optional subject, which means that pupils have to state at the beginning of the school year if they wish to attend religious instruction classes.

Only qualified persons who have been approved by the competent authority of the church or religious society in question may be appointed as teachers of religious instruction (§ 3 of the RelUG). Should the authorisation of the church or religious society be withdrawn, the teacher may no longer be employed as a teacher in religious education classes (§ 6 of the RelUG). For teachers employed by a church or religious community, withdrawal constitutes a reason for the termination of their employment.

The organisation, implementation and direct control of religious education classes are the responsibility of the church or religious society in question. The state has the right to supervise religious instruction in organisational and disciplinary ways by means of its school supervisory bodies (§ 2 section 2 of the RelUG). Therefore, it is the religious society and not the state which organises religious instruction classes, despite the fact that religious instruction as a compulsory subject enjoys equal standing with other subjects. These regulations apply to public schools and private schools with public status.

15 See chapter2.1.

16 Cf. the contributions in Rinnerthaler, Alfred (ed.), *Historische und rechtliche Aspekte des Religionsunterrichts* (Frankfurt am Main et al.: Peter Lang, 2004).

The design of the curricula for religious education are the responsibility of churches and religious societies; the Ministry of Education must be informed and must publish them in the Federal Law Gazette (*Bundesgesetzblatt*), though this is merely of declaratory significance.[17] State approval is not necessary. One restriction is the requirement that only such books and teaching materials may be used that are not in conflict with the aim of educating responsible citizens (§ 3 section 2 of the RelUG).

Textbooks for religious instruction classes are included in the schoolbook programme in accordance with the Act on Equalisation of Family Burdens 1967 (*Familienlastenausgleichgesetz*, FLAG)[18] and are financed by the state.

12.5.2 *The Establishment of Islamic Religious Instruction*

Since the introduction of Islamic religious instruction in Austrian public schools in 1983, the school administration has faced several problems, though the system works well on the whole. In 1998, the Islamic Religious Pedagogical Academy, established according to the regulations for pedagogical academies under the Austrian Private School Act (PrivSchG), was founded. This was adopted in the interests of the Islamic community and the Austrian school administration. Meanwhile, the legal foundation of this Academy has been changed according to the Federal Act on the Organisation of the Pedagogical Colleges and their Studies of 2005 (*Bundesgesetz über die Organisation der Pädagogischen Hochschulen und ihre Studien*, HochschulG).[19] In the 2006/2007 academic year the research department of "Islamic Religious Pedagogy" was established at the University of Vienna. Its main task is the instruction of teachers of religious education in secondary high schools.

Bundesgesetz vom 13. Juli 1949, betreffend den Religionsunterricht in der Schule (ReligionsunterrichtsG)
BGBl. Nr. 190/1949 as amended BGBl. Nr. 256/1993

§ 1

(1) Für alle Schüler, die einer gesetzlich anerkannten Kirche oder Religionsgesellschaft angehören, ist der Religionsunterricht ihres Bekenntnis-

17 Lehrpläne für den islamischen Religionsunterricht an Pflichtschulen, mittleren und höheren Schulen BGBl. II Nr. 234/2011.

18 BGBl. Nr. 376/1967 as amended BGBl. I Nr. 104/2019.

19 BGBl. I Nr. 30/2006 as amended BGBl. I Nr. 101/2018.

ses Pflichtgegenstand an den öffentlichen und den mit dem Öffentlichkeitsrecht ausgestatteten
a) Volks-, Haupt- und Sonderschulen,
b) Polytechnischen Lehrgängen,
c) allgemeinbildenden höheren Schulen,
d) berufsbildenden mittleren und höheren Schulen (einschließlich der land- und forstwirtschaftlichen Schulen),
e) Berufsschulen in den Bundesländern Tirol und Vorarlberg sowie land- und forstwirtschaftliche Berufsschulen im gesamten Bundesgebiet,
f) Akademien für Sozialarbeit
g) Anstalten der Lehrer- und Erzieherbildung (einschließlich der land- und forstwirtschaftlichen Lehranstalten), wobei an den Pädagogischen, Berufspädagogischen und Land- und forstwirtschaftlichen berufspädagogischen Akademien an die Stelle des Religionsunterrichts der Unterricht in Religionspädagogik tritt und in den folgenden Bestimmungen unter Religionsunterricht auch Religionspädagogik zu verstehen ist.
(2) Schüler, die das 14. Lebensjahr noch nicht vollendet haben, können jedoch von ihren Eltern zu Beginn eines jeden Schuljahres von der Teilnahme am Religionsunterricht schriftlich abgemeldet werden; Schüler über 14 Jahren können eine solche schriftliche Abmeldung selbst vornehmen.
(3) An den öffentlichen und mit dem Öffentlichkeitsrecht ausgestatteten Berufsschulen, soweit sie nicht unter Abs. 1 lit. e fallen, ist für alle Schüler, die einer gesetzlich anerkannten Kirche oder Religionsgesellschaft angehören, der Religionsunterricht ihres Bekenntnisses als Freigegenstand zu führen.

§ 2

(1) Der Religionsunterricht wird durch die betreffende gesetzlich anerkannte Kirche oder Religionsgemeinschaft besorgt, geleitet und unmittelbar beaufsichtigt. Dem Bund steht jedoch—soweit § 7d nicht anderes bestimmt—das Recht zu, durch seine Schulaufsichtsorgane den Religionsunterricht in organisatorischer und schuldisziplinärer Hinsicht zu beaufsichtigen.
(2) Die Lehrpläne für den Religionsunterricht werden hinsichtlich des Lehrstoffes und seiner Aufteilung auf die einzelnen Schulstufen von der betreffenden gesetzlich anerkannten Kirche oder Religionsgesellschaft im Rahmen der staatlich festgesetzten Wochenstundenzahl für den Religionsunterricht erlassen und sodann—soweit § 7d nicht anderes be-

stimmt—vom zuständigen Bundesminister bekanntgemacht. Den gesetzlich anerkannten Kirchen und Religionsgesellschaften ist vor der Festsetzung und vor jeder Änderung der Wochenstundenanzahl für den Religionsunterricht Gelegenheit zur Stellungnahme zu geben.
(3) Für den Religionsunterricht dürfen nur Lehrbücher und Lehrmittel verwendet werden, die nicht im Widerspruch zur staatsbürgerlichen Erziehung stehen.

§ 2a

(1) Die Teilnahme an den von den gesetzlich anerkannten Kirchen und Religionsgesellschaften zu besonderen Anlässen des schulischen oder staatlichen Lebens, insbesondere zu Beginn und am Ende des Schuljahres abgehaltenen Schülergottesdiensten sowie die Teilnahme an religiösen Übungen oder Veranstaltungen ist den Lehrern und Schülern freigestellt.
(2) Den Schülern ist zur Teilnahme an den im Abs. 1 genannten Schülergottesdiensten und religiösen Übungen oder Veranstaltungen die Erlaubnis zum Fernbleiben vom Unterricht im bisherigen Ausmaß zu erteilen.

§ 2b

(1) In den unter § 1 Abs. 1 fallenden Schulen, an denen die Mehrzahl der Schüler einem christlichen Religionsbekenntnis angehört, ist in allen Klassenräumen vom Schulerhalter ein Kreuz anzubringen.
(2) Die Bestimmung des Abs. 1 gilt hinsichtlich jener Schularten, bezüglich deren Erhaltung dem Bund die Grundsatzgesetzgebung und den Ländern die Ausführungsgesetzgebung zukommt, als Grundsatzbestimmung.
(3) Hinsichtlich jener Schulen, bezüglich deren Erhaltung die Gesetzgebung ausschließlich den Ländern zukommt, bleibt die Regelung der im Abs. 1 behandelten Frage der Landesgesetzgebung vorbehalten.

§ 3

(1) Die Religionslehrer an den öffentlichen Schulen, an denen Religionsunterricht Pflichtgegenstand oder Freigegenstand ist, werden entweder
a) von der Gebietskörperschaft (Bund, Länder), die die Diensthoheit über die Lehrer der entsprechenden Schulen ausübt, angestellt oder
b) von der betreffenden gesetzlich anerkannten Kirche oder Religionsgesellschaft bestellt.

(2) Die Anzahl der Lehrerstellen, die gemäß Abs. 1 lit. a besetzt werden, bestimmt die Gebietskörperschaft auf Antrag der zuständigen kirchlichen (religionsgesellschaftlichen) Behörde.
(3) Alle Religionslehrer unterstehen hinsichtlich der Vermittlung des Lehrgutes des Religionsunterrichtes den Vorschriften des Lehrplanes und den kirchlichen (religionsgesellschaftlichen) Vorschriften und Anordnungen; im übrigen unterstehen sie in der Ausübung ihrer Lehrtätigkeit den allgemeinen staatlichen schulrechtlichen Vorschriften.
(4) …

§ 4

(1) Die gemäß § 3 Abs. 1 lit. a von den Gebietskörperschaften (Bund, Länder) angestellten Religionslehrer sind Bedienstete der betreffenden Gebietskörperschaft. Auf sie finden die für die Lehrer an den betreffenden öffentlichen Schulen geltenden Vorschriften des Dienstrechtes einschließlich des Besoldungsrechtes und, sofern es sich um Religionslehrer handelt, die zu der Gebietskörperschaft in einem öffentlich-rechtlichen Dienstverhältnis stehen, auch einschließlich des Pensions- und des Disziplinarrechtes unter Bedachtnahme auf die Bestimmungen der folgenden Abs. 2 bis 5 Anwendung.
(2) Die Gebietskörperschaften (Bund, Länder) dürfen nur solche Personen als Religionslehrer anstellen, die von der zuständigen kirchlichen (religionsgesellschaftlichen) Behörde als hiezu befähigt und ermächtigt erklärt sind. Vor Aufnahme in das öffentlich-rechtliche Dienstverhältnis als Religionslehrer und vor Verleihung einer schulfesten Stelle an einen Religionslehrer ist die zuständige kirchliche (religionsgesellschaftliche) Behörde zu hören.
(3) Wird einem unter Abs. 1 fallenden Religionslehrer die ihm erteilte Ermächtigung (Abs. 2) nach erfolgter Anstellung von der zuständigen kirchlichen (religionsgesellschaftlichen) Behörde entzogen, so darf er für die Erteilung des Religionsunterrichtes nicht mehr verwendet werden.
(4) Bei einem als Vertragsbediensteten angestellten Religionslehrer gilt der Entzug der kirchlichen (religionsgesellschaftlichen) Ermächtigung für den Dienstgeber als Kündigungsgrund, sofern nicht nach den Vorschriften des Vertragsbedienstetenrechtes zugleich ein Grund zur Entlassung oder für eine sonstige vorzeitige Auflösung des Dienstverhältnisses vorliegt.
(5) Wird einem im öffentlich-rechtlichen Dienstverhältnis angestellten Religionslehrer die kirchliche (religionsgesellschaftliche) Ermächtigung

entzogen, so ist er, wenn nicht zugleich ein Austritt aus dem Dienstverhältnis oder ein auf Entlassung lautendes Disziplinarerkenntnis oder ein den Verlust des Amtes zur Folge habendes rechtskräftiges strafgerichtliches Urteil vorliegt, oder sofern er nicht nach den allgemeinen Bestimmungen des Dienstrechtes wegen Dienstunfähigkeit—wobei der Entzug der kirchlichen (religionsgesellschaftlichen) Ermächtigung als solcher nicht als Dienstunfähigkeit gilt—oder wegen seines Alters in den dauernden Ruhestand versetzt wird oder wegen Erreichung der Altersgrenze von Gesetzes wegen in den dauernden Ruhestand tritt, aus dem öffentlich-rechtlichen Dienstverhältnis unter Bedachtnahme auf die sozialversicherungsrechtlichen Vorschriften auszuscheiden und so zu behandeln, als ob er Vertragsbediensteter wäre (Abs. 4); hiebei sind die für die Erlangung höherer Bezüge angerechneten Vordienstzeiten hinsichtlich der Höhe des Monatsentgeltes zu berücksichtigen.

§ 5

(1) Die gemäß § 3 Abs. 1 lit. b von den gesetzlich anerkannten Kirchen und Religionsgesellschaften bestellten Religionslehrer müssen die österreichische Staatsbürgerschaft besitzen und—außer dem Erfordernis der kirchlich (religionsgesellschaftlich) erklärten Befähigung und Ermächtigung für die Erteilung des Religionsunterrichtes—hinsichtlich der Vorbildung die besonderen Anstellungserfordernisse erfüllen, die für die im § 3 Abs. 1 lit. a genannten Religionslehrer gelten. In besonders begründeten Ausnahmefällen kann—soweit § 7d nicht anderes bestimmt—der zuständige Bundesminister von dem Erfordernis der österreichischen Staatsbürgerschaft Nachsicht erteilen.
(2) Durch die Bestellung dieser Religionslehrer wird ein Dienstverhältnis zu den Gebietskörperschaften (Bund, Länder) nicht begründet.

§ 6

(1) Die im § 3 Abs. 1 lit. b genannten Religionslehrer erhalten für ihre Lehrtätigkeit an öffentlichen Schulen eine Vergütung nach den Ansätzen des Entlohnungsschemas II L (§ 44 des Vertragsbedienstetengesetzes 1948, BGBl. Nr. 86, in seiner jeweils geltenden Fassung) zuzüglich der jeweiligen Bezugszuschläge, nach den für die Lehrer der betreffenden Schularten dort festgesetzten Entlohnungsgruppen.
(2) Im übrigen finden hinsichtlich der Bemessung der Vergütung für die im § 3 Abs. 1 lit. b genannten Religionslehrer die Bestimmungen des Ver-

tragsbedienstetengesetzes 1948, BGBl. Nr. 86, in seiner jeweils geltenden Fassung, soweit sie sich auf Vertragsbedienstete des Entlohnungsschemas II L beziehen, dem Sinne nach—insbesondere hinsichtlich Dauer des Dienstverhältnisses, Kündigung, Abfertigung, Entlassung, Erkrankung, Todesfall—Anwendung. Desgleichen haben diese Religionslehrer Anspruch auf Vergütung nach den für die Vertragsbediensteten des Bundes jeweils geltenden Reisegebührenvorschriften mit der Maßgabe, daß bei Religionslehrern, die Geistliche oder Ordensangehörige oder Angehörige von Diakonissenanstalten sind, der Wohnort als Dienstort gilt.

§ 7

Den Aufwand für die im § 6 angeführten Vergütungen trägt die Gebietskörperschaft (Bund, Länder), die nach Maßgabe der bundesgesetzlichen Vorschriften die Kosten der Besoldung der übrigen Lehrer an der betreffenden Schule trägt.

§ 7a

(1) Nehmen am Religionsunterricht eines Bekenntnisses weniger als die Hälfte der Schüler einer Klasse teil, so können die Schüler dieses Bekenntnisses mit Schülern desselben Bekenntnisses von anderen Klassen oder Schulen (derselben Schulart oder verschiedener Schularten) zu Religionsunterrichtsgruppen zusammengezogen werden, soweit dies vom Standpunkt der Schulorganisation und des Religionsunterrichtes vertretbar ist.
(2) Nehmen am Religionsunterricht eines Bekenntnisses in einer Klasse weniger als 10 Schüler teil, die zugleich weniger als die Hälfte der Schüler dieser Klasse sind, oder nehmen am Religionsunterricht in einer Religionsunterrichtsgruppe weniger als 10 Schüler teil, die in ihren Klassen jeweils weniger als die Hälfte der Schüler jeder einzelnen Klasse sind, so vermindert sich die festgesetzte Wochenstundenanzahl für den Religionsunterricht (§ 2 Abs. 2), sofern sie mehr als eine Stunde beträgt, auf die Hälfte, mindestens jedoch auf eine Wochenstunde; diese Verminderung tritt nicht ein, wenn der Lehrerpersonalaufwand für die Erteilung des Religionsunterrichtes hinsichtlich der Differenz auf das volle Wochenstundenausmaß von der betreffenden gesetzlich anerkannten Kirche oder Religionsgesellschaft getragen wird.
(3) Nehmen am Religionsunterricht eines Bekenntnisses in einer Klasse vier oder drei Schüler teil, die zugleich weniger als die Hälfte der Schüler

dieser Klasse sind, oder nehmen am Religionsunterricht in einer Religionsunterrichtsgruppe vier oder drei Schüler teil, die in ihren Klassen jeweils weniger als die Hälfte der Schüler jeder einzelnen Klasse sind, und konnte durch Zusammenziehung der Schüler gemäß Abs. 1 keine höhere Zahl erreicht werden, so beträgt die Wochenstundenanzahl für den Religionsunterricht (§ 2 Abs. 2) eine Wochenstunde; diese Verminderung tritt nicht ein, wenn der Lehrerpersonalaufwand für die Erteilung des Religionsunterrichtes hinsichtlich der Differenz auf das volle Wochenstundenausmaß von der betreffenden gesetzlich anerkannten Kirche oder Religionsgesellschaft getragen wird. In diesen Fällen gebühren den Religionslehrern nur die Bezahlung für eine Wochenstunde, nicht jedoch sonstige Vergütungen für finanzielle und zeitliche Aufwendungen für die im Zusammenhang mit der Erteilung dieses Religionsunterrichtes allenfalls erforderlichen Reisebewegungen.
(4) Ein Religionsunterricht für weniger als drei Schüler einer Klasse, die zugleich weniger als die Hälfte der Schüler dieser Klasse sind, sowie ein Religionsunterricht für weniger als drei Schüler einer Religionsunterrichtsgruppe, die in ihren Klassen jeweils weniger als die Hälfte der Schüler jeder einzelnen Klasse sind, ist im vollen oder in dem in den Abs. 2 oder 3 angeführten verminderten Wochenstundenausmaß nur dann zu erteilen, wenn die betreffende gesetzlich anerkannte Kirche oder Religionsgesellschaft den Lehrerpersonalaufwand hiefür trägt.
(5) Die Absätze 1 bis 4 finden keine Anwendung auf Religion als Wahlpflichtgegenstand an allgemeinbildenden höheren Schulen im Sinne des § 39 Abs. 1 Z 3 lit. b des Schulorganisationsgesetzes, BGBl. Nr. 242/1962, in der Fassung des Bundesgesetzes BGBl. Nr. 327/1988.

§ 7b

(1) Als Religionslehrer an den unter § 1 fallenden mit dem Öffentlichkeitsrecht ausgestatteten und sonstigen privaten Schulen dürfen nur Personen verwendet werden, die von der zuständigen kirchlichen (religionsgesellschaftlichen) Behörde als hiezu befähigt und ermächtigt erklärt sind. Wird einem solchen Religionslehrer die ihm erteilte Ermächtigung von der zuständigen kirchlichen (religionsgesellschaftlichen) Behörde entzogen, so darf er für die Erteilung des Religionsunterrichtes nicht mehr verwendet werden.[20]

20 Cf. the case law to § 132 section 4 of the ArbVG, below chapter 15.4.

(2) Auf die im Abs. 1 genannten Religionslehrer finden die Bestimmungen des § 3 Abs. 3 sowie sinngemäß die Bestimmungen des § 4 Abs. 4 und 5 Anwendung; ferner finden auf die im Abs. 1 genannten Schulen die Bestimmungen des § 7a sinngemäß Anwendung.

§ 7c

(1) Für die unmittelbare Beaufsichtigung des Religionsunterrichtes (§ 2 Abs. 1) werden von den gesetzlich anerkannten Kirchen und Religionsgesellschaften Fachinspektoren für den Religionsunterricht bestellt.[21]
(2) Durch die Bestellung zum Fachinspektor für den Religionsunterricht wird weder ein eigenes Dienstverhältnis zu den Gebietskörperschaften (Bund, Länder) begründet noch ein auf Grund der Anstellung als Religionslehrer (§ 3 Abs. 1 lit. a) bestehendes Dienstverhältnis zu einer Gebietskörperschaft (Bund, Länder) berührt.
(3) Religionslehrern (§ 3 Abs. 1), die zu Fachinspektoren für den Religionsunterricht bestellt werden, ist, soweit sie unter die nach Abs. 4 festzusetzende Zahl fallen, für ihre Tätigkeit als Religionsinspektoren die nötige Lehrpflichtermäßigung oder Lehrpflichtbefreiung unter Belassung ihrer vollen Bezüge beziehungsweise ihrer vollen Vergütung zu gewähren. Außerdem ist ihnen nach den Grundsätzen, die für die Dienstzulagen der Fachinspektoren für einzelne Gegenstände gelten (§ 71 Abs. 2 des Gehaltsgesetzes 1956, BGBl. Nr. 54), ein Verwendungszuschuß in gleicher Höhe und erforderlichenfalls ein Reisekostenpauschale nach den für die Fachinspektoren für einzelne Gegenstände geltenden Grundsätzen zu gewähren. Der Verwendungszuschuß ist bei den als Fachinspektoren für den Religionsunterricht verwendeten Religionslehrern, die als Religionslehrer im öffentlich-rechtlichen Dienstverhältnis zu einer Gebietskörperschaft (Bund, Länder) stehen, nach den für die Dienstzulagen der Fachinspektoren für einzelne Gegenstände geltenden Grundsätzen (§ 71 Abs. 3 des Gehaltsgesetzes 1956, BGBl. Nr. 54) für die Bemessung des Ruhegenusses anrechenbar. Der aus den Bestimmungen dieses Absatzes sich ergebende Aufwand einschließlich der Vertretungskosten für die zu Fachinspektoren für den Religionsunterricht bestellten Religionslehrer ist entsprechend den Bestimmungen über den Personalaufwand für die Beamten des Schulaufsichtsdienstes vom Bund zu tragen.

21 At present eight inspectors for Islamic religious education are appointed by the IGGÖ.

(4) Die Zahl der Fachinspektoren für den Religionsunterricht, auf die die Bestimmungen des Abs. 3 Anwendung finden, wird auf Antrag der zuständigen kirchlichen (religionsgesellschaftlichen) Behörden
– soweit es sich nicht um land- und forstwirtschaftliche Schulen handelt, nach Anhörung des zuständigen Landesschulrats—vom zuständigen Bundesminister im Einvernehmen mit dem Bundeskanzler
– soweit § 7d nicht anderes bestimmt—festgesetzt.

…

§ 9

(1) Dieses Bundesgesetz tritt in jedem Bundesland mit dem 1. jenes Monates in Kraft, der der Kundmachung des mit diesem Bundesgesetze übereinstimmenden Landesgesetzes des betreffenden Bundeslandes nachfolgt, die Bestimmungen des § 3, Abs. (1) und Abs. (2), lit. a, sowie der § § 4, 6 und 7 jedoch nicht vor dem 1. Jänner 1950.
(2) § 7c Abs. 4 in der Fassung des Bundesgesetzes BGBl. Nr. 256/1993 tritt mit 1. Juli 1993 in Kraft.

§ 10

(1) Mit der Vollziehung dieses Bundesgesetzes, soweit sie in den Wirkungsbereich des Bundes fällt, sowie mit der Wahrnehmung der Rechte des Bundes gemäß Art. 14 Abs. 8 und 14a Abs. 6 des Bundes-Verfassungsgesetzes in der Fassung von 1929 ist der Bundesminister für Unterricht, Kunst und Sport betraut, soweit Abs. 2 nicht anderes bestimmt.
(2) Mit der die land- und forstwirtschaftlichen Schulen des Bundes betreffenden Vollziehung des § 2b Abs. 1 und der dienst- und besoldungsrechtlichen Bestimmungen dieses Bundesgesetzes für die Religionslehrer sowie mit der Wahrnehmung der Rechte des Bundes gemäß Art. 14a Abs. 6 des Bundes-Verfassungsgesetzes in der Fassung von 1929 hinsichtlich der dienst- und besoldungsrechtlichen Bestimmungen dieses Bundesgesetzes für Religionslehrer an sonstigen land- und forstwirtschaftlichen Schulen ist der Bundesminister für Land- und Forstwirtschaft betraut.

…

12.6 Islamic Private Schools

In accordance with Article 17 section 2 of the StGG 1867,[22] the establishment and running of private schools and other educational institutions is guaranteed provided their legal qualifications can be approved. Systematically seen, like the right to religious instruction, this article also concretises the parents' right to have their religious or philosophical convictions respected and the children's right to education in accordance with Article 2 of Additional Protocol 1 to the ECHR.

Apart from special provisions concerning the establishment, maintenance and closure of schools, in principle the state school law also applies to private schools. However, there are a few exemptions. For instance, school admission based on a private contract between the school's operators and the pupils or their parents is one. Such contractual agreements allow for a certain freedom of arrangements within the compulsory state law, such as the membership of certain confessions, school fees, or other reasons for termination of the contractual relationship.

Schools which are operated by legally recognised churches or religious societies or by trusts or funds recognised by them are known as denominational private schools (*konfessionelle Privatschulen*); certain special regulations apply to them. Private schools are granted public status, which empowers them to issue school reports legally equivalent to those of state-run schools of the same type, if their operators, heads and teachers can guarantee proper and regular instruction in accordance with the aims of Austrian schooling. If private schools are operated by legally recognised churches and religious societies, the fulfilment of those conditions is legally presumed (§ 14 section 3 of the PrivSchG). This legal presumption does not apply to private schools run by other religious communities or any other private entities, so the conditions for the achievement of public status must be approved in every single case.

In the case of legally prescribed school types, the results achieved in class must be equivalent to those in a state school of the same type (sustainable operation in conformity with the tasks of the public-school system). The fulfilment of these conditions is legally presumed in the case of recognised churches and religious societies (§ 11 section 3 of the PrivSchG).

Only schools operated by legally recognised churches or religious societies are granted subsidies towards the costs of teaching personnel for denominational private schools with public status, the so-called "living subsidies" (§ 17 of

22 See chapter 2.1.

the PrivSchG). This means that the teachers needed by denominational schools to meet the requirements of the school curriculum are employed and paid by the competent state governing body, not by the relevant religious society. Both the teacher concerned and the competent authority in the church or religious society have to agree to the teacher's appointment to the denominational school as a corollary of the right to religious freedom in its individual and organisational dimension. This also means that the employment of a teacher must be terminated if his or her consent or that of the religious authority in question no longer exists. In exceptional cases, instead of a "living subsidy" an equivalent financial subsidy may be granted for the deployment of teachers provided by the relevant religious society.

Bundesgesetz vom 25. Juli 1962 über das Privatschulwesen (Privatschulgesetz—PrivSchG),
BGBl. Nr. 244/1962 as amended BGBl. I Nr. 71/2008

§ 1—*Geltungsbereich*

Dieses Bundesgesetz regelt die Errichtung und Führung von Privatschulen—mit Ausnahme der land- und forstwirtschaftlichen Schulen—sowie die Verleihung des Öffentlichkeitsrechtes und die Gewährung von Subventionen an solche Privatschulen.

§ 2—*Begriffsbestimmungen*

(1) Schulen im Sinne dieses Bundesgesetzes sind Einrichtungen, in denen eine Mehrzahl von Schülern gemeinsam nach einem festen Lehrplan unterrichtet wird, wenn im Zusammenhang mit der Vermittlung von allgemeinbildenden oder berufsbildenden Kenntnissen und Fertigkeiten ein erzieherisches Ziel angestrebt wird.
(2) Ein erzieherisches Ziel ist gegeben, wenn außer den mit der Erwerbung von Kenntnissen und Fertigkeiten an sich verbundenen Erziehungszielen die Festigung der charakterlichen Anlagen der Schüler in sittlicher Hinsicht bezweckt wird.
(3) Privatschulen sind Schulen, die von anderen als den gesetzlichen Schulerhaltern errichtet und erhalten werden (Artikel 14 Abs. 6 und 7 des Bundes-Verfassungsgesetzes in der Fassung von 1929 und in der Fassung des Bundesverfassungsgesetzes vom 18. Juli 1962, BGBl. Nr. 215).
(4) Eine Lehrbefähigung im Sinne dieses Bundesgesetzes liegt bei Erfüllung der für ein öffentlich-rechtliches oder ein privatrechtliches Dienst-

verhältnis erforderlichen besonderen Ernennungs- bzw. Anstellungserfordernisse vor.

§ 2a

Österreichischen Staatsbürgern und inländischen juristischen Personen sind Staatsangehörige und juristische Personen eines Landes, dessen Angehörigen und juristischen Personen Österreich auf Grund eines Staatsvertrages im Rahmen der europäischen Integration dieselben Rechte zu gewähren hat wie Inländern und inländischen juristischen Personen, gleichgestellt.

ABSCHNITT I—*Errichtung und Führung von Privatschulen*

§ 3—*Voraussetzungen für die Errichtung*

(1) Die Errichtung von Privatschulen ist im Sinne des Artikels 17 Abs. 2 des Staatsgrundgesetzes vom 21. Dezember 1867, RGBl. Nr. 142, über die allgemeinen Rechte der Staatsbürger, und—soweit es sich um Schulen von gesetzlich anerkannten Kirchen oder Religionsgesellschaften handelt—auch im Sinne des § 4 des Gesetzes vom 25. Mai 1868, RGBl. Nr. 48, wodurch grundsätzliche Bestimmungen über das Verhältnis der Schule zur Kirche erlassen werden,[23] bei Erfüllung der in diesem Bundesgesetz enthaltenen näheren Vorschriften gewährleistet.
(2) Die Errichtung von Privatschulen setzt voraus, daß die Bedingungen hinsichtlich des Schulerhalters (§ 4), der Leiter und Lehrer (§ 5) und der Schulräume und Lehrmittel (§ 6) erfüllt werden.

§ 4—*Schulerhalter*

(1) Eine Privatschule zu errichten, ist als Schulerhalter—bei Erfüllung der sonstigen in diesem Abschnitt festgesetzten Voraussetzungen—berechtigt
a) jeder österreichische Staatsbürger, der voll handlungsfähig ist, der in sittlicher Hinsicht verläßlich ist und in dessen Person keine Umstände vorliegen, die nachteilige Auswirkungen auf das österreichische Schulwesen erwarten lassen;

23 See chapter 12.3.

b) jede Gebietskörperschaft, gesetzlich anerkannte Kirche oder Religionsgesellschaft und sonstige Körperschaft des öffentlichen Rechts;
c) jede sonstige inländische juristische Person, deren vertretungsbefugte Organe die Voraussetzungen nach lit. a erfüllen.
(2) Andere als österreichische Staatsbürger und andere als inländische juristische Personen können als Schulerhalter—bei Erfüllung der sonstigen in diesem Abschnitt festgesetzten Voraussetzungen—Privatschulen errichten, wenn sie beziehungsweise ihre vertretungsbefugten Organe in sittlicher Hinsicht verläßlich und keine nachteiligen Auswirkungen auf das österreichische Schulwesen zu erwarten sind. Sofern die vertretungsbefugten Organe nicht die österreichische Staatsbürgerschaft besitzen und ihren Wohnsitz nicht in Österreich haben, ist von ausländischen juristischen Personen ein Zustellungsbevollmächtigter zu bestellen, der die österreichische Staatsbürgerschaft besitzt und seinen Wohnsitz in Österreich hat. Durch Staatsverträge (Kulturabkommen) begründete Rechte werden hiedurch nicht berührt.
(3) Aufgabe des Schulerhalters ist die finanzielle, personelle und räumliche Vorsorge für die Führung der Schule.
(4) Der Schulerhalter hat außer den ihm nach diesem Bundesgesetz sonst obliegenden Anzeigen jede nach den Bestimmungen dieses Bundesgesetzes maßgebende Veränderung in seiner Person beziehungsweise in der Person seiner vertretungsbefugten Organe und in der Organisation der Schule sowie die Einstellung der Schulführung und die Auflassung der Schule der zuständigen Schulbehörde unverzüglich anzuzeigen und ihr auf Verlangen alle zur Wahrnehmung der Aufsicht (§ 22) erforderlichen Auskünfte über die Schule zu geben. Er darf den Organen der zuständigen Schulbehörden den Zutritt zu den Schulliegenschaften, die Beobachtung des Unterrichtes und die Einsicht in die Schulakten nicht verweigern.
(5) Der Schulerhalter hat sich der Einflußnahme auf die nach den schulrechtlichen Vorschriften dem Leiter der Schule—sofern er nicht selbst Leiter der Schule ist (§ 5 Abs. 2)—und den Lehrern zukommenden Aufgaben zu enthalten.

§ 5—*Leiter und Lehrer*

(1) Für die pädagogische und schuladministrative Leitung der Privatschule ist ein Leiter zu bestellen,
a) der die österreichische Staatsbürgerschaft besitzt,
b) der die Eignung zum Lehrer in sittlicher und gesundheitlicher Hinsicht aufweist,

c) der die Lehrbefähigung für die betreffende oder eine verwandte Schulart oder eine sonstige geeignete Befähigung nachweist und
d) in dessen Person keine Umstände vorliegen, die nachteilige Auswirkungen auf das österreichische Schulwesen erwarten lassen.
(2) Schulerhalter, welche die im Abs. 1 lit. a bis c genannten Bedingungen erfüllen, können die Leitung der Privatschule auch selbst ausüben.
(3) Der Leiter ist für die unmittelbare Leitung und Überwachung des Unterrichtes an der Privatschule verantwortlich. Er ist an die in Ausübung der Aufsicht (§ 22) erteilten Weisungen der zuständigen Schulbehörden gebunden.
(4) Die an der Schule verwendeten Lehrer haben ebenfalls die im Abs. 1 lit. a bis d genannten Bedingungen zu erfüllen.
(5) Die zuständige Schulbehörde kann von dem Erfordernis der österreichischen Staatsbürgerschaft (Abs. 1 lit. a und Abs. 4) Nachsicht erteilen, wenn die Verwendung im Interesse der Schule gelegen ist und öffentliche Interessen der Nachsichterteilung nicht entgegenstehen.
(6) Die Bestellung des Leiters und der Lehrer sowie jede nach den Bestimmungen dieses Bundesgesetzes maßgebende Veränderung in deren Person ist vom Schulerhalter der zuständigen Schulbehörde unverzüglich anzuzeigen, welche die Verwendung des Leiters oder Lehrers innerhalb eines Monats ab dem Einlangen der Anzeige zu untersagen hat, wenn die Bedingungen der vorstehenden Absätze nicht erfüllt sind. Darüber hinaus hat die zuständige Schulbehörde die Verwendung eines Leiters oder Lehrers zu untersagen, wenn die in den vorstehenden Absätzen genannten Bedingungen später wegfallen, sowie hinsichtlich des Leiters auch dann, wenn er die ihm nach Abs. 3 obliegenden Aufgaben nicht ausreichend erfüllt.
(7) Die Bestimmungen des Abs. 6 gelten sinngemäß auch für den Schulerhalter in seiner Eigenschaft als Leiter der Schule (Abs. 2).

§ 6—*Schulräume und Lehrmittel*

Der Schulerhalter hat nachzuweisen, daß er über Schulräume verfügt, die baulich und einrichtungsmäßig dem Zweck und der Organisation der Privatschule sowie den Grundsätzen der Pädagogik und der Schulhygiene entsprechen. Ferner hat er nachzuweisen, daß die Privatschule die zur Durchführung des Lehrplanes notwendigen Lehrmittel und sonstigen Ausstattungen und Einrichtungen aufweist.

§ 7—*Anzeige und Untersagung der Errichtung*

(1) Die Errichtung einer Privatschule ist der zuständigen Schulbehörde mindestens drei Monate vor der beabsichtigten Eröffnung der Schule unter Nachweis der Erfüllung der Bestimmungen des § 4 Abs. 1 oder 2, des § 5 Abs. 1 oder 2 und 4 (unbeschadet der Bestimmung des § 5 Abs. 5) sowie des § 6 anzuzeigen.
(2) Die zuständige Schulbehörde hat die Errichtung der Schule binnen zwei Monaten ab dem Zeitpunkt der Einbringung der Anzeige zu untersagen, wenn die im Abs. 1 angeführten Bestimmungen nicht erfüllt sind. Wird die Errichtung der Schule innerhalb dieser Frist nicht untersagt, so kann sie eröffnet werden.

§ 8—*Erlöschen und Entzug des Rechtes zur Schulführung*

(1) Das Recht zur Führung einer Schule erlischt
a) mit der Auflassung der Schule durch den Schulerhalter,
b) mit dem Wegfall einer der im § 4 Abs. 1 oder 2 genannten Bedingungen,
c) nach Ablauf eines Jahres, in dem die Schule nicht geführt wurde,
d) mit der Überlassung des Schulvermögens an eine andere Person in der Absicht, die Schulerhalterschaft aufzugeben, oder
e) mit dem Tode des Schulerhalters (bei juristischen Personen mit deren Auflösung); die Verlassenschaft beziehungsweise die Erben des Schulerhalters können die Schule jedoch bis zum Ende des laufenden Schuljahres weiterführen, wobei sie die Rechte und Pflichten des Schulerhalters übernehmen; sie haben die Weiterführung der Schule der zuständigen Schulbehörde anzuzeigen.
(2) Werden nach der Eröffnung der Schule die im § 5 Abs. 1, 2 oder 4 (unter allfälliger Bedachtnahme auf § 5 Abs. 5) oder im § 6 genannten Bedingungen nicht mehr erfüllt, so hat die zuständige Schulbehörde dem Schulerhalter eine angemessene Frist zur Beseitigung der Mängel zu setzen. Werden die Mängel innerhalb dieser Frist nicht behoben, so hat die Schulbehörde die weitere Führung der Schule zu untersagen.
(3) Wenn für die Gesundheit oder Sittlichkeit der Schüler Gefahr im Verzug ist, hat die zuständige Schulbehörde die weitere Führung der Schule ohne Setzung einer Frist zu untersagen.

§ 9—*Bezeichnung von Privatschulen*

Jede Privatschule hat eine Bezeichnung zu führen, aus der ihr Schulerhalter erkennbar ist und die, auch wenn die Schule das Öffentlichkeitsrecht (Abschnitt III) besitzt, jede Möglichkeit einer Verwechslung mit einer öffentlichen Schule ausschließt. Wenn nicht eine Bewilligung zur Führung einer gesetzlich geregelten Schulartbezeichnung nach Abschnitt II erteilt worden ist, muß ferner jede Verwechslungsmöglichkeit mit einer solchen Bezeichnung ausgeschlossen sein.

§ 10—*Schülerheime*

(1) Die Errichtung privater Heime, in die Schüler öffentlicher oder privater Schulen zum Zwecke des Schulbesuches oder zur Überwachung ihrer Lerntätigkeit aufgenommen werden (Schülerheime), bedarf keiner Anzeige.
(2) Die zuständige Schulbehörde hat die Führung eines Schülerheimes zu untersagen, wenn trotz Aufforderung zur Abstellung von Mängeln innerhalb einer angemessenen Frist weiterhin Umstände vorliegen, durch die für die Gesundheit, die Sittlichkeit oder die staatsbürgerliche Gesinnung der Schüler Gefahr besteht. Diese Untersagung gilt für die Dauer des Vorliegens der festgestellten Mängel.

ABSCHNITT II—*Führung einer gesetzlich geregelten Schulartbezeichnung*

§ 11—*Bewilligungspflicht*

(1) Die Führung einer gesetzlich geregelten Schulartbezeichnung durch Privatschulen ist nur mit Bewilligung der zuständigen Schulbehörde zulässig.
(2) Die Bewilligung ist auf Ansuchen des Schulerhalters zu erteilen, wenn
a) die Organisation einschließlich des Lehrplanes und die Ausstattung der Privatschule im wesentlichen mit gleichartigen öffentlichen Schulen übereinstimmt und an der Schule nur schulbehördlich approbierte Lehrbücher, soweit eine solche Approbation vorgesehen ist, verwendet werden,
b) der Leiter und die Lehrer die Lehrbefähigung für die betreffende Schulart besitzen, wobei jedoch die zuständige Schulbehörde vom Nachweis der Lehrbefähigung für Lehrer absehen kann, wenn Mangel an entsprechend lehrbefähigten Lehrern besteht und ein sonstiger ausreichender Befähigungsnachweis erbracht wird, und

c) glaubhaft gemacht wird, daß die Führung der Privatschule für mehrere Jahre mit einem hohen Grad der Wahrscheinlichkeit sichergestellt ist.
(3) Bei Gebietskörperschaften, gesetzlich anerkannten Kirchen und Religionsgesellschaften und sonstigen Körperschaften des öffentlichen Rechts wird die Erfüllung der Voraussetzungen des Abs. 2 lit. c von Gesetzes wegen angenommen.
(4) Um die Bewilligung zur Führung einer gesetzlich geregelten Schulartbezeichnung kann gleichzeitig mit der Anzeige der Errichtung der Privatschule (§ 7) angesucht werden.

§ 12—*Widerruf der Bewilligung*

Werden die im § 11 Abs. 2 genannten Voraussetzungen nicht mehr voll erfüllt, so hat die zuständige Schulbehörde dem Schulerhalter eine angemessene Frist zur Beseitigung der Mängel zu setzen. Werden die Mängel innerhalb dieser Frist nicht behoben, so hat die Schulbehörde die Bewilligung zur Führung einer gesetzlich geregelten Schulartbezeichnung zu widerrufen, sofern nicht § 8 anzuwenden ist.

ABSCHNITT III—*Öffentlichkeitsrecht*

§ 13—*Rechtswirkungen des Öffentlichkeitsrechtes*

(1) Durch die Verleihung des Öffentlichkeitsrechtes wird einer Privatschule das Recht übertragen, Zeugnisse über den Erfolg des Schulbesuches auszustellen, die mit der Beweiskraft öffentlicher Urkunden und mit den gleichen Rechtswirkungen ausgestattet sind wie Zeugnisse gleichartiger öffentlicher Schulen.
(2) Mit dem Öffentlichkeitsrecht sind weiters folgende Rechtswirkungen verbunden:
a) an der Schule können die für die betreffende Schulart vorgesehenen Prüfungen abgehalten werden;
b) der Schule können Lehramtsanwärter, die sich damit einverstanden erklären, zur Einführung in die Praxis des Lehramtes mit Zustimmung des Schulerhalters zugewiesen werden;
c) auf die Schule finden die für die entsprechenden öffentlichen Schulen geltenden schulrechtlichen Vorschriften Anwendung, soweit gesetzlich nicht anderes bestimmt ist und soweit sie nicht die Errichtung, Erhaltung und Auflassung, die Sprengel und das Schulgeld betreffen. Bei der Anwendung von landesgesetzlichen Vorschriften betreffend die äußere

Organisation der öffentlichen Pflichtschulen treten an die Stelle der dort vorgesehenen Behördenzuständigkeiten jene des § 23.

§ 14—*Verleihung des Öffentlichkeitsrechtes*

(1) Privatschulen, die gemäß § 11 eine gesetzlich geregelte Schulartbezeichnung führen, ist das Öffentlichkeitsrecht zu verleihen, wenn
a) der Schulerhalter (bei juristischen Personen dessen vertretungsbefugte Organe), der Leiter und die Lehrer Gewähr für einen ordnungsgemäßen und den Aufgaben des österreichischen Schulwesens gerecht werdenden Unterricht bieten und
b) der Unterrichtserfolg jenem an einer gleichartigen öffentlichen Schule entspricht.
(2) Privatschulen, die keiner öffentlichen Schulart entsprechen, ist das Öffentlichkeitsrecht zu verleihen, wenn
a) die Voraussetzungen nach Abs. 1 lit. a vorliegen,
b) die Organisation, der Lehrplan und die Ausstattung der Schule sowie die Lehrbefähigung des Leiters und der Lehrer mit einem vom Bundesminister für Unterricht, Kunst und Kultur erlassenen oder genehmigten Organisationsstatut übereinstimmen und
c) die Privatschule sich hinsichtlich ihrer Unterrichtserfolge bewährt hat.
(3) Bei Gebietskörperschaften, gesetzlich anerkannten Kirchen und Religionsgesellschaften und sonstigen Körperschaften des öffentlichen Rechts wird die Erfüllung der Voraussetzungen des Abs. 1 lit. a und des Abs. 2 lit. a von Gesetzes wegen angenommen.

Case Law

Case 1: In accordance with its constitution, the IGGÖ, through the training of religious teachers, pastoral workers and religious servants, is ensuring the preservation and cultivation of religion among the followers of Islam. Since, in the "internal affairs" of the legally recognised churches and religious societies, the state organs are deprived of all authority over legislation and enforcement by Article 15 of the StGG, the state school authorities have no responsibility for the approval of a private school operating in these matters pursuant to § 14 section 2 of the PrivSchG without the consent of the IGGÖ: VwGH 31. 1. 2005, 2002/10/0015.

§ 15—*Dauer der Verleihung*

Das Öffentlichkeitsrecht darf an Privatschulen vor ihrem lehrplanmäßig vollen Ausbau jeweils nur für die bestehenden Klassen (Jahresstufen) und jeweils nur für ein Schuljahr verliehen werden. Nach Erreichung des lehrplanmäßig vollen Ausbaues kann das Öffentlichkeitsrecht nach Maßgabe der Unterrichtserfolge auch auf mehrere Schuljahre verliehen werden. Wenn Gewähr für eine fortdauernde Erfüllung der gesetzlichen Bedingungen besteht, ist das Öffentlichkeitsrecht nach Erreichung des lehrplanmäßig vollen Ausbaues der Schule auf die Dauer der Erfüllung der gesetzlichen Bedingungen zu verleihen.

§ 16—*Entzug und Erlöschen des Öffentlichkeitsrechtes*

(1) Wenn die im § 14 genannten Voraussetzungen während der Dauer des Öffentlichkeitsrechtes nicht mehr voll erfüllt werden, ist dem Schulerhalter unter Androhung des Entzuges beziehungsweise der Nichtweiterverleihung des Öffentlichkeitsrechtes eine Frist bis längstens zum Ende des darauffolgenden Schuljahres zur Behebung der Mängel zu setzen. Werden die Mängel innerhalb der gesetzten Frist nicht behoben, so ist das Öffentlichkeitsrecht zu entziehen beziehungsweise nicht weiterzuverleihen.
(2) Mit der Auflassung einer Privatschule erlischt das ihr verliehene Öffentlichkeitsrecht. In diesem Falle sind die an der Schule geführten Amtsschriften und Kataloge der zuständigen Schulbehörde zur Aufbewahrung zu übergeben.

ABSCHNITT IV—*Subventionierung von Privatschulen*

A. *Subventionierung konfessioneller Privatschulen*

§ 17—*Anspruchsberechtigung*

(1) Den gesetzlich anerkannten Kirchen und Religionsgesellschaften sind für die mit dem Öffentlichkeitsrecht ausgestatteten konfessionellen Privatschulen nach Maßgabe der folgenden Bestimmungen Subventionen zum Personalaufwand zu gewähren.
(2) Unter konfessionellen Privatschulen sind die von den gesetzlich anerkannten Kirchen und Religionsgesellschaften und von ihren Einrichtungen erhaltenen Schulen sowie jene von Vereinen, Stiftungen und Fonds

erhaltenen Schulen zu verstehen, die von der zuständigen kirchlichen (religionsgesellschaftlichen) Oberbehörde als konfessionelle Schulen anerkannt werden.

§ 18—*Ausmaß der Subventionen*

(1) Als Subvention sind den gesetzlich anerkannten Kirchen und Religionsgesellschaften für die konfessionellen Schulen jene Lehrerdienstposten zur Verfügung zu stellen, die zur Erfüllung des Lehrplanes der betreffenden Schule erforderlich sind (einschließlich des Schulleiters und der von den Lehrern an vergleichbaren öffentlichen Schulen zu erbringenden Nebenleistungen), soweit das Verhältnis zwischen der Zahl der Schüler und der Zahl der Lehrer der betreffenden konfessionellen Schule im wesentlichen jenem an öffentlichen Schulen gleicher oder vergleichbarer Art und vergleichbarer örtlicher Lage entspricht.
(2) Die gemäß Abs. 1 den einzelnen konfessionellen Schulen zukommenden Lehrerdienstposten hat die zuständige Schulbehörde auf Antrag der für die Schule entsprechend dem § 17 Abs. 2 in Betracht kommenden Kirche oder Religionsgesellschaft festzustellen.
(3) Die gesetzlich anerkannte Kirche oder Religionsgesellschaft hat Umstände, die eine Auswirkung auf die Anzahl der einer konfessionellen Schule zukommenden Lehrerdienstposten zur Folge haben können, unverzüglich der zuständigen Schulbehörde zu melden.
(4) Die zuständige Schulbehörde hat bei Änderung der Voraussetzungen nach Abs. 1 die Anzahl der der Schule zukommenden Lehrerdienstposten neu festzustellen.
(5) Wenn für eine konfessionelle Schule
a) erstmals um das Öffentlichkeitsrecht angesucht wurde oder
b) im vorangegangenen Schuljahr das Öffentlichkeitsrecht verliehen und nicht gemäß § 16 Abs. 1 entzogen worden ist sowie für das laufende Schuljahr um die Verleihung des Öffentlichkeitsrechtes angesucht wurde,
ist sie hinsichtlich der Subventionierung auf Antrag der betreffenden gesetzlich anerkannten Kirche oder Religionsgesellschaft so zu behandeln, als ob ihr das Öffentlichkeitsrecht bereits verliehen worden wäre. Wird das Öffentlichkeitsrecht jedoch nicht verliehen, so hat die gesetzlich anerkannte Kirche oder Religionsgesellschaft dem Bund den durch die Subventionierung entstandenen Aufwand zu ersetzen.
(6) Die Feststellung der den einzelnen konfessionellen Schulen zukommenden Lehrerdienstposten wird mit Beginn des auf die Einbringung des Antrages gemäß Abs. 2 und die Änderung der maßgeblichen Voraus-

setzungen folgenden Monatsersten wirksam, sofern der Antrag jedoch für ein bevorstehendes Schuljahr oder einen bevorstehenden Teil eines Schuljahres vorgelegt wird, frühestens mit Beginn des Schuljahres beziehungsweise des Teiles des Schuljahres.

§ 19—*Art der Subventionierung*

(1) Die Subventionen zum Personalaufwand sind nach Maßgabe der Bestimmungen dieses Abschnittes zu gewähren:
a) durch Zuweisung von Bundeslehrer oder Bundesvertragslehrern durch den Bund als lebende Subventionen an die Schule, soweit es sich nicht um eine in lit. b genannte Schule handelt, oder
b) durch Zuweisung von Landeslehrern oder Landesvertragslehrern durch das Land als lebende Subventionen an Volks-, Haupt- und Sonderschulen, polytechnische Lehrgänge und Berufsschulen.
(2) Die Kosten der Subventionen zum Personalaufwand sind auch in den Fällen des Abs. 1 lit. b vom Bund zu tragen.
(3) Ist die Zuweisung eines Lehrers nach Abs. 1 nicht möglich, so hat der Bund für den unterrichtenden Lehrer eine Vergütung in der Höhe der Entlohnung zu leisten, die diesem Lehrer zustehen würde, wenn er entsprechend der Art der betreffenden Schule entweder Bundes- oder Landesvertragslehrer wäre. Erfüllt dieser Lehrer die Anstellungserfordernisse nicht, ist die Vergütung in der Höhe der Entlohnung festzusetzen, die in gleichartigen Fällen in der Regel Bundes(Landes)vertragslehrern gegeben wird. Der Bund hat auch die für einen solchen Lehrer für den Dienstgeber auf Grund gesetzlicher Vorschriften anfallenden Leistungen bis zu der der Vergütung entsprechenden Höhe zu ersetzen. Durch die Zahlung der Vergütung wird ein Dienstverhältnis zum Bund nicht begründet.
(4) Die Vergütung gemäß Abs. 3 ist an den unterrichtenden Lehrer auszuzahlen. Sofern der Lehrer jedoch Angehöriger eines Ordens oder einer Kongregation der katholischen Kirche ist und die Schule, an der er unterrichtet, von diesem Orden oder dieser Kongregation erhalten wird, ist die Vergütung an den Schulerhalter zu zahlen.
(5) Wird einer konfessionellen Schule das Öffentlichkeitsrecht rückwirkend verliehen und wurde kein Antrag gemäß § 18 Abs. 5 gestellt, ist der in Betracht kommenden gesetzlich anerkannten Kirche oder Religionsgesellschaft für diese Schule der Lehrerpersonalaufwand zu ersetzen, den der Schulerhalter für die dort unterrichtenden Lehrer geleistet hat, höchstens jedoch im Ausmaß des Betrages, der bei Anwendung der Abs. 3 und 4 bezahlt worden wäre.

§ 20—*Grenzen der Zuweisung lebender Subventionen*

(1) Den unter § 17 fallenden Schulen dürfen nur solche Lehrer als lebende Subventionen zugewiesen werden, die sich damit einverstanden erklären und deren Zuweisung an die betreffende Schule die zuständige kirchliche (religionsgesellschaftliche) Oberbehörde beantragt oder gegen deren Zuweisung sie keinen Einwand erhebt.
(2) Die Zuweisung ist aufzuheben, wenn der Lehrer dies beantragt oder wenn die zuständige kirchliche (religionsgesellschaftliche) Oberbehörde die weitere Verwendung des Lehrers an der betreffenden Schule aus religiösen Gründen für untragbar erklärt und aus diesem Grunde die Aufhebung der Zuweisung bei der zuständigen Dienstbehörde beantragt.

B. *Subventionierung sonstiger Privatschulen*
…

ABSCHNITT V—*Gemeinsame Bestimmungen*

§ 22—*Aufsicht über die Privatschulen*
(1) Die Aufsicht über die Privatschulen erstreckt sich auf die Überwachung der Erfüllung der Bestimmungen des Abschnittes I, bei Privatschulen, die zur Führung einer gesetzlich geregelten Schulartbezeichnung berechtigt sind, auch auf die Überwachung der Erfüllung der Bestimmungen des Abschnittes II und bei Privatschulen mit Öffentlichkeitsrecht überdies auf die Überwachung der Erfüllung der Bestimmungen des Abschnittes III.
(2) Die Aufsicht über private Schülerheime erstreckt sich auf die im § 10 Abs. 2 vorgesehenen Maßnahmen.

…

§ 24—*Strafbestimmungen*

Wer entgegen den Bestimmungen dieses Bundesgesetzes
a) eine Privatschule ohne Anzeige oder nach Untersagung der Errichtung eröffnet; oder nach Entzug oder Erlöschen des Rechtes zur Führung einer Privatschule diese weiterführt;
b) für eine Privatschule eine Bezeichnung führt, die mit der Bezeichnung einer öffentlichen Schule verwechslungsfähig ähnlich ist; oder für eine Privatschule ohne Öffentlichkeitsrecht den Anschein erweckt, als ob sie das Öffentlichkeitsrecht besitze;

oder ohne Bewilligung eine gesetzlich geregelte Schulartbezeichnung oder eine mit dieser verwechslungsfähig ähnliche Bezeichnung führt;
c) Zeugnisse ausstellt, die mit den Zeugnissen einer öffentlichen oder mit dem Öffentlichkeitsrecht ausgestatteten Schule gleich oder verwechslungsfähig ähnlich sind, ohne daß die Schule das Öffentlichkeitsrecht besitzt;
d) einen Leiter oder Lehrer nach der Untersagung dessen Verwendung weiter in dieser Eigenschaft an der Schule beschäftigt;
e) den Organen der zuständigen Schulbehörden den Zutritt zu den Schulliegenschaften, die Beobachtung des Unterrichts und die Einsicht in die Schulakten ungerechtfertigterweise verweigert oder die nach den Bestimmungen dieses Bundesgesetzes zu erstattenden Anzeigen oder Auskünfte unterläßt;
f) ein privates Schülerheim nach Untersagung der Führung trotz weiteren Vorliegens der beanständeten Mängel weiterführt,
begeht, wenn die Tat nicht nach anderen gesetzlichen Vorschriften strenger zu bestrafen ist, eine Verwaltungsübertretung und ist von der Bezirksverwaltungsbehörde mit einer Geldstrafe bis zu 2 180 Euro, im Falle der Uneinbringlichkeit mit Ersatzfreiheitsstrafe bis zu vier Wochen zu bestrafen.

CHAPTER 13

Islam in Tertiary Educational Institutions

13.1 Islamic Religious Teacher Education

The Federal Act on the Organisation of the Pedagogical Colleges and their Studies of 2005 (HochschulG)[1] ensures the independent incorporation of the "Teachers' Training Academies" into the tertiary education sector including the bachelor's degree as a condition for teaching appointments. The legislator—as highlighted in the Explanatory Notes to the HochschulG—has taken into account that the subject matter of religious instruction as well as teachers' training falls within the ambit of the "internal affairs" of the legally recognised churches and religious societies. Therefore, the right to religious freedom comes into effect primarily as far as the curricula are concerned. With respect to the fact that denominational colleges are private institutions, the legal relationship with their students is based on a contract under private law. Regarding the structure and organisation of the colleges, the same quality and academic level as provided at public institutions must be guaranteed. As a consequence, denominational colleges are obliged to observe the general provisions concerning the qualifications of teaching staff including performance review, academic autonomy, student co-determination and allowance for previous studies, personnel and material equipment. Among the general leading principles, the development of social competence in connection with the imparting of social, moral-ethical and religious values is explicitly mentioned. In order to ensure the comparability of these studies and degrees with those of the public Teachers' Training Colleges, the law provides for recognition proceedings (§§4–7 of the HochschulG).

The IGGÖ and the AGÖ have concluded agreements with the Ecclesiastical Pedagogical College (*Kirchliche Pädagogische Hochschule*), which offers curricula for the education of teachers of religious instruction.[2] There are also cooperation agreements regarding religious teachers' education with the Israelite Religious Society and the Buddhist Religious Society. Based on these

1 Cf. Chapter 12, fn. 19.

2 An Ecumenical Board has been set up for the Christian denominations (Protestant, Orthodox, Old-Catholic, Eastern-Oriental and Free Churches) at the Viennese Catholic College.

agreements, Islamic Institute[3] and an Alevi Institute have been set up at that College.[4]

Bundesgesetz über die Organisation der Pädagogischen Hochschulen und ihre Studien (HochschulG 2005)
BGBl. I Nr. 30/2006 as amended BGBl. I Nr. 101/2018
…
§ 7

(1) Anerkannte Bildungseinrichtungen sind zur Führung der Bezeichnung „Private Pädagogische Hochschule" berechtigt. Anerkannte Studienangebote sind als „Private Hochschullehrgänge" zu bezeichnen.
(2) Für anerkannte private Pädagogische Hochschulen und anerkannte private Hochschullehrgänge gemäß Abs. 1 gelten die Bestimmungen der Abschnitte 1 bis 5 des 2. Hauptstücks. Gegen Entscheidungen ist eine Beschwerde an das Bundesverwaltungsgericht zulässig.
(3) Private Pädagogische Hochschulen sowie private Hochschullehrgänge unterliegen der Aufsicht des zuständigen Regierungsmitglieds (§ 24).
(3a) Die Curricula oder deren Teile für den Erwerb der Lehrbefähigung für den Unterrichtsgegenstand Religion sind im Sinne von Art. 15 StGG durch die anerkannten konfessionellen privaten Pädagogischen Hochschulen zu erlassen und haben in ihren Grundsätzen und in ihrer Qualität den Bestimmungen dieses Bundesgesetzes zu entsprechen.
(4) Konfessionellen privaten Pädagogischen Hochschulen sind die zur Erfüllung der Aufgaben nach diesem Bundesgesetz erforderlichen Subventionen zum Personalaufwand des Lehrpersonals (einschließlich der Aus-, Fort- und Weiterbildung der Religionslehrer) wie sie dem Aufwand öffentlicher Pädagogischer Hochschulen vergleichbarer Art und Größe entsprechen, zu gewähren.
(5) Die Subventionierung kann dabei durch die Zuweisung von Planstellen sowie durch die Bereitstellung von Mitteln für Leistungen Dritter, wie sie öffentlichen Pädagogischen Hochschulen für personalkapazitätswirksame Leistungen zur Verfügung stehen, erfolgen.
(6) Im Bereich der Fort- und Weiterbildung sind die zur Erfüllung dieser Aufgaben erforderlichen Subventionen zum Personalaufwand des Lehr-

3 https://www.kphvie.ac.at/institute/institut-islamische-religion.html [last accessed 24 March 2020].
4 https://www.kphvie.ac.at/institute/institut-alevitische-religion.html [last accessed 24 March 2020].

personals unter sinngemäßer Anwendung der §§ 30 und 31 nach Maßgabe einer jährlich im Einvernehmen mit dem zuständigen Regierungsmitglied festzulegenden Planung zu gewähren. Dies gilt nicht für die religionspädagogische Fort- und Weiterbildung.
…

13.2 Islamic Theology and Religious Pedagogics at State Universities

The Austrian constitutional system contains no explicit guarantee of theological research at state universities or academies.[5] Although the constitutional foundations of the law on schools presuppose the existence of religious instruction in public schools, in principle the state has no obligation to provide for the training of teachers of religious education, because the legally recognised churches and religious societies and not the state are the entrepreneurs of religious instruction. There is, therefore, no constitutional obligation for the state to integrate theology in the canon of subjects of research and teaching at universities. Nonetheless, an overall view of the constitutional principles of the law on religion shows that fulfilling this task is in absolute conformity with the constitutional system in Austria.

Basically, the training of spiritual personnel as well as the whole of office and employment law belongs to the "internal affairs" of the legally recognised churches and religious societies in accordance with Article 15 of the StGG. Therefore, the state itself cannot take over the training of spiritual personnel. However, an appropriate state education such as is provided in theological faculties can be approved by the churches and religious societies.

It is not clear whether the Islamic religious society entrusts the research and teaching of theology to the state universities. § 24 section 1 of the IslamG shows that the Islamic religious societies have in principle agreed to recognise and accept graduates of state universities in the fields of theology and religious pedagogy into their service.

There is no challenge to the guarantee of freedom of teaching and science if the specific nature of theology is considered within the framework of state universities. To cultivate the scientific field of religion without including theo-

5 Potz, Richard, 'Islamische Theologie an der Universität', in Haering, Stephan, et. al. (eds.), *In mandatis meditari, Festschrift für Hans Paarhammer* (Berlin: Duncker & Humblot, 2012), 929–950; Hammer, Stefan, "Zur konfessionellen Bindung der Theologie aus Sicht der Wissenschaftsfreiheit," in Schinkele, Brigitte, et al. (eds.), *Recht—Religion—Kultur. Festschrift für Richard Potz* (Vienna: facultas.wuv, 2014), 117–132.

logy would be a questionable loss from the point of view of social politics as well as science politics. The organisation of theological research and teaching at state universities, however, must take four interacting aspects into account: the religious and ideological neutrality of the state, the self-determination of the religious communities, the guarantees for teaching and research, as well as the fundamental rights of the theologians concerned.

The introduction of regular studies in Islamic theology in addition to the study of Islamic religious pedagogy at the University of Vienna was a particular innovation of the IslamG 2015.[6] In accordance with § 24 section 1 up to six jobs for teaching staff were provided for the purpose of theological research and teaching and to ensure the academic education of spiritual ministers of Islamic religious societies.[7]

In accordance with § 24 section 3 of the IslamG a separate branch of study (*Studienzweig*) must be provided for each Islamic religious society.[8] On the occasion of the appointment of a professorship provided for in this Act, the Rector of the University of Vienna must contact (*Fühlungnahme*) the Islamic religious societies regarding the persons proposed as candidates. Thereby, it must be taken into consideration that the persons teaching theological core subjects are adherents of a religious doctrine (Islamic law school) represented in the Islamic religious societies recognised under this Act (§ 24 section 4).

Masterstudium „Islamische Religionspädagogik“,
Mitteilungsblatt der Universität Wien vom 25.06.2012, 36. Stück, Nummer 242 as amended 02.02.2016, 13. Stück, Nummer 97[9]

Präambel
Das Masterstudium „Islamische Religionspädagogik“ der Universität Wien hat die Intention, islamische Religionslehrerinnen und Religions-

6 Potz, Richard, fn. 146.

7 In the 2019/2020 winter term four professorial positions were occupied: those in Islamic Religious Pedagogics, Law and Ethics in Islam, Alevitic-Theological Studies and Islam in Contemporary Society.

8 However, the term *Studienzweig* for a specialisation is unknown in the field of study law. Therefore, this provision could lead to some further problems in the future: for instance, if the number of Islamic religious societies increases owing to the division of an existing Islamic religious society or the recognition of a further Islamic religious society. A second, and already actual, question is the treatment of Alevite theology, which is quite different from Islamic theology, so that instead of treating it as a specialisation within Islamic theology a special field of study would be needed.

9 http://www.univie.ac.at/mtbl02/2006_2007/112.pdf [last accessed 24 March 2020].

lehrer für höhere Schulen in Österreich auszubilden. Zusätzlich wird auf Themen und aktuelle Fragestellungen religiöser und ethischer Bildung in Forschung und Lehre eingegangen. Die Durchführung des Curriculums erfolgt in enger Zusammenarbeit mit den facheinschlägigen Instituten der theologischen Fakultäten der Universität Wien, sowie mit allen weiteren Forschungseinrichtungen und Personen, die einschlägige Leistungen in Forschung und Lehre erbringen.

Bachelorstudium „Islamisch-Theologische Studien" der Universität Wien mit dem Schwerpunkt a) Islamische Religionspädagogik, dem Schwerpunkt b) Islamische Theologie und dem Schwerpunkt c) Alevitisch-Theologische Studien
Mitteilungsblatt UG 2002 vom 26.06.2017, 31. Stück, Nummer 153, as amended Mitteilungsblatt UG 2002 vom 14.06.2019, 26. Stück, Nummer 216[10]

Präambel
Das Bachelorstudium „Islamisch-Theologische Studien" der Universität Wien mit dem Schwerpunkt a) Islamische Religionspädagogik, dem Schwerpunkt b) Islamische Theologie und dem Schwerpunkt c) Alevitisch-Theologische Studien hat als bekenntnisorientiertes und interdisziplinäres Fach die Intention, einen Beitrag zur Entwicklung einer Tradition der Islamischen Theologie und Studien auf der europäischen universitären Ebene zu leisten und arbeitet mit anderen wissenschaftlichen Disziplinen eng zusammen. Das islamisch-theologische Wissen wird unter den Bedingungen österreichischer Universitäten und durch den akademischen Diskurs nicht nur verwaltet und an die Studierenden weitergegeben, sondern reflexiv ausgelegt, bearbeitet und weiterentwickelt. Dabei geht es vor allem einerseits um die reflexive und wissenschaftliche Aufarbeitung der islamisch-theologischen Traditionen sowie der Rekonstruktion und Kritik der Methoden und Theorien der einzelnen Disziplinen der Islamischen Theologie, um die Methoden, Lehren und Theorien in einen neuen Kontext zu stellen und sie damit zu aktualisieren. Andererseits bezieht sich ihre kritische Reflexion auch auf den kulturellen, sozialen und politischen Kontext, in dem sie agiert, um herkömmliche polare Denkschemata und konstruierte Gegensätze zu vermeiden. Die Islamisch-Theologischen Studien befassen sich insbesondere auch mit

10 https://mtbl.univie.ac.at/storage/media/mtbl02/02_pdf/20190614-26.pdf [last accessed 24 March 2020].

den verschiedenen innerislamischen Lehrmeinungen und Strömungen in ihrer Pluralität und Heterogenität. Somit leisten die Islamisch-Theologischen Studien auch einen Beitrag zum innerislamischen Dialog. Darüber hinaus tragen die Islamisch-Theologischen Studien zur Versachlichung der Debatten über den Islam bei und sorgen dafür, dass neue Prägungen des Islam unter den neuen Verhältnissen und Bedingungen in Europa entstehen. Dabei soll eine wissenschaftliche Auseinandersetzung mit den aktuellen globalen Diskursen im Bereich der Islamischen Theologie stattfinden. Durch die Verankerung von Alternativen Pflichtmodulen/Pflichtmodulgruppen soll für Studierende die Möglichkeit geschaffen werden, sich im jeweils gewählten Bereich zu vertiefen.
...

13.3 Private Universities

The Act Concerning Studies at Academies and Establishing Colleges for Pedagogical Professions (Universitätsakkreditierungsgesetz, UniAkkG) of 1999, replaced in 2011 by the Act on Private Universities (*Privatuniversitätengesetz*, PUG),[11] put an end to the state monopoly in Austria and made the organisation of private universities possible. However, there are currently no Islamic private universities under Austrian patronage.

11 BGBl. I Nr. 74/2011 as amended BGBl. I Nr. 31/2018.

CHAPTER 14

Special Pastoral Care

14.1 Introduction

The field of religious services and pastoral care must be seen in terms of both the individual and the right to religious freedom. Rules regarding the individual dimension are contained in the laws for the institutions concerned. They are a consequence of the interpretation of fundamental rights using a more substantial approach, encompassing a certain state obligation to take measures to ensure the practice of religious freedom even under difficult circumstances. Any form of religious assistance which the religious communities are permitted to provide may be carried out only in the form of an offer without any manner of compulsion being used.

The organisational dimension is included in the special laws for the legally recognised churches and religious societies. Therefore, §§ 11 and 19 of the IslamG[1] contain concrete provisions which guarantee pastoral care in the armed forces as well as in hospitals and prisons.

14.2 Chaplaincy in Healthcare Institutions

The Federal Act on Hospitals and Healthcare Institutions (*Krankenanstalten- und Kuranstaltengesetz*, KaKuG)[2] describes the patient's right to pastoral care on demand (§ 5a no. 5). According to the distribution of competences between the *Bund* and the *Bundesländer*, the latter must ensure that the administrators of hospitals and healthcare institutions comply with this legal duty, taking into account the specific purpose of the institution in question. This precept has been regularly implemented in all individual laws of the *Bundesländer* together with the right to psychological support. This reflects the legislator's endeavour to provide for the comprehensive care of patients.

In principle, hospitals may ask patients to state their religious affiliation before admission. However, this is a crucial issue insofar as there is at the same time no explicit obligation to inform the patient that he or she actually has

1 See chapter 3.
2 BGBl. Nr. 1/1957 as amended BGBl. I Nr. 14/2019.

the right to refuse to answer this question. In practice, one may assume that this will be handled differently. However, it must be emphasised that informing the patient in advance is the only fully consistent way to deal with the negative dimension of the right to religious freedom. The problem in question has resulted in a controversial debate, particularly with regard to data protection.

Apart from occasional minimal personnel, subsidies on the basis of regional provisions, pastoral care in healthcare institutions is not financed by the state, although its infrastructure is financed to some degree.

14.3 Chaplaincy in Prisons

The individual's right to practise his or her religion in penal institutions is governed by § 85 of the Act on Imprisonment (*Strafvollzugsgesetz*, StVG).[3] This guarantee includes the prisoner's right to attend services or other religious events of his or her "own confession" usually held in the institution. Moreover, communication with a pastoral advisor, who is appointed or admitted to the institution concerned, at reasonable intervals must be guaranteed. On a case by case basis, after having heard the pastoral advisor, a prisoner can be excluded from participating in worship or other religious ceremonies for reasons of security or the requirements of the prison regime. If a pastoral advisor of the inmate's confession is neither appointed nor admitted and the prisoner asks for pastoral care, the prison governor is obliged to nominate a spiritual advisor from the relevant religious community, insofar as this is possible in the particular circumstances.

With respect to Roman-Catholic pastoral care in prisons, financial provision has been made for a small number of official positions for pastoral advisors, who are engaged on an employment contract basis and financed by the state. According to special agreements, a small amount is given to the Evangelical Church and the Islamic Religious Society in Austria.

Bundesgesetz vom 26. März 1969 über den Vollzug der Freiheitsstrafen und der mit Freiheitsentziehung verbundenen vorbeugenden Maßnahmen (Strafvollzugsgesetz—StVG)
BGBl. Nr. 144/169 as amended BGBl. I Nr. 100/2018

3 BGBl. Nr. 144/1969 as amended BGBl. I Nr. 100/2018.

§ 85—*Seelsorge*

(1) Jeder Strafgefangene hat das Recht, in der Anstalt am gemeinschaftlichen Gottesdienst und an anderen gemeinsamen religiösen Veranstaltungen teilzunehmen und Heilsmittel sowie den Zuspruch eines an der Anstalt bestellten oder zugelassenen Seelsorgers zu empfangen. Der Anstaltsleiter kann aus Gründen der Sicherheit und Ordnung nach Anhörung des Seelsorgers Strafgefangene von der Teilnahme am Gottesdienst und an anderen Veranstaltungen ausschließen.
(2) Einem Strafgefangenen ist auf sein ernstliches Verlangen auch zu gestatten, in der Anstalt den Zuspruch eines nicht für die Anstalt bestellten oder zugelassenen Seelsorgers seines eigenen Bekenntnisses zu empfangen. Die Entscheidung hierüber steht dem Anstaltsleiter zu.
(3) Ist in der Anstalt für ein Bekenntnis ein Seelsorger weder bestellt noch zugelassen, so ist dem Strafgefangenen auf sein Verlangen nach Möglichkeit ein Seelsorger namhaft zu machen, an den er sich wenden kann. Diesem ist der Besuch des Strafgefangenen zu dessen seelsorgerischer Betreuung zu gestatten.
(4) Strafgefangenen ist zu gestatten, auch außerhalb der Besuchszeiten (§ 94 Abs. 1) während der Amtsstunden den Besuch eines Seelsorgers zu empfangen. Der Inhalt der zwischen dem Strafgefangenen und dem Seelsorger geführten Gespräche ist nicht zu überwachen. Im übrigen gelten für solche Besuche die §§ 94 und 95 dem Sinne nach.

14.4 Chaplaincy in the Armed Forces

The tradition of pastoral care for Muslims in Austrian armed forces dates back to the chaplaincy for Bosnian military units in the Austro-Hungarian monarchy.[4] Two military imams are currently active in the Islamic military chaplaincy established in 2015.[5]

The financing of personnel expenses and material expenditure for chaplaincies in the armed forces is regularly set out in the special laws. In fact, hitherto

4 Organised military pastoral care for Muslim soldiers in Bosnian units has existed since 1881. The Provisional Defence Act for Bosnia and Herzegovina contained detailed rules for Muslim soldiers. In 1914 a military mufti was established based on the model of a Catholic military bishop.

5 See also the provisions regarding the religious obligations of Muslim members of the army (prayer, Islamic meals, fasting etc.), below in chapter 16.2.1.

the wages and expenses have been fully state-financed only for the Catholic Church and the Protestant Church. As regards other churches and religious societies, only small reimbursements for expenses have so far been provided for.

CHAPTER 15

Employment and Social Law

15.1 Introduction

Religion has to be considered in different ways in the legal order of employment relations. By reason of the guarantee of religious freedom the religious beliefs of employees must be taken into account as well as the religious orientation of employers, especially of religious communities and their bodies, who can also rely on their religious freedom.

This dual nature of the religious dimension in employment law is also reflected in anti-discrimination law, which on the one hand protects employees from religious discrimination, and on the other contains an exemption clause for occupational activities within churches and other organisations, especially to protect the ethos on which religion or belief is based (Article 4 section 2 of Directive 2000/78/EC).

Furthermore, provisions regarding religious holidays and a provision in the Act concerning the Employment of Foreigners within the Federal Territory[1] belong to the area of religion and employment law.

15.2 Employment Contract

Religiously motivated activities can, in principle, be the subject of an employment contract in accordance with civil law (cf. § 1151 ABGB). Within the freedom of employment contracts, religious communities have the opportunity to implement their genuine *proprium* as regards the services delivered inside their institutions. Thus, state law can be modified as regards optional law, and even compulsory labour law must be interpreted in the light of the right to self-determination (Article 15 of the StGG).

§ 36 section 2 no. 6 of the Act on Labour Constitution (ArbVG) excludes people whose activities are characterised mainly by religious, welfare or social purposes from the definition of employees if they are not employed under an employment contract. This is the case when the special motivation outweighs

1 See chapter 8.

the usual economic objectives of the employment. Thus, voluntary and honorary workers are not employees as prescribed by law.

Bundesgesetz vom 14. Dezember 1973 betreffend die Arbeitsverfassung (Arbeitsverfassungsgesetz—ArbVG)
BGBl. Nr. 22/1974 as amended BGBl. I Nr. 23/2020

…
§ 36—*Arbeitnehmerbegriff*

(1) Arbeitnehmer im Sinne des II. Teiles sind alle im Rahmen eines Betriebes beschäftigten Personen einschließlich der Lehrlinge und der Heimarbeiter ohne Unterschied des Alters.
(2) Als Arbeitnehmer gelten nicht:
[…]
6. Personen, deren Beschäftigung vorwiegend durch religiöse, karitative oder soziale Motive bestimmt ist, sofern sie nicht auf Grund eines Arbeitsvertrages beschäftigt sind

15.3 Manifestations of Religion by Employees

Employees' religious observance can have different effects. As almost all religions have holidays and "holy times," it is primarily working time regulations that are affected.[2] Moreover, some religions practise restrictions in the form of taboos, as do Muslims the handling of alcohol and pork, which could create problems, especially in gastronomy and the food industry.[3] Finally, religious rules on conduct and clothing can also be affected; currently the most prominent example is the wearing at work of the Islamic headscarf.[4]

15.4 Religiously Orientated Employers

In accordance with § 132 section 1 of the ArbVG some provisions regarding the participation of a works council in economic decision-making, which could

2 See chapter 15.6.
3 Such difficulties for Muslim employees are sometimes reported in the media, but hitherto no conflict has found its way to court.
4 See chapter 17.

weaken the specific purpose of the institution, are wholly or partly inapplicable to businesses and enterprises which directly serve political, coalitional-political, denominational, scientific, educational or welfare purposes (tendency protection/*Tendenzschutz*).

In accordance with § 132 section 4, 1st sentence of the ArbVG the provisions regarding works constitutions do not apply to companies that serve the denominational purposes of a legally recognised church or religious society, insofar as they are in conflict with the specific nature of the company (so-called extended *Tendenzschutz*). Consequently, each case must be examined individually in order to determine whether the provision is compatible with the specific nature resulting from the right to self-determination of the church or religious society in question. This provision should be understood as a realisation of the constitutionally guaranteed autonomy of churches and religious societies on the level of sub-constitutional law in the field of labour law.

In accordance with § 132 section 4, 2nd sentence of the ArbVG, several provisions of this Act are by no means applicable to enterprises and administrative organisations charged with the administration of the "internal affairs" of legally recognised churches and religious societies, in practice company agreements on certain matters, rights to economic information, intervention and consultation, as well as, to some extent, the right to be involved in operative changes.

In particular, the corresponding limited application of the ArbVG is of practical relevance to personnel matters concerning those staff members in charge of activities directly involving denominational purposes. In principle, conflicts between a church or religious society and its officials in matters of private law employment contracts may be taken to court. However, all preliminary questions, for instance the validity of the removal from office, retirement, disciplinary measures, transfer to another place of work or function etc., are excluded from the court's assessment. Thereby, according to the established case law, the courts make no distinction as to whether or not the impugned conduct is directly connected with the specific purposes of the enterprise.

Against this background and through the integration into national law of the European anti-discrimination law, one can assume that the established special concept of grading loyalties owed by employees to denominational employers according to the employers' self-understanding will essentially continue to endure as far as pastoral, teaching and leading functions are concerned.

Bundesgesetz vom 14. Dezember 1973 betreffend die Arbeitsverfassung (Arbeitsverfassungsgesetz—ArbVG)
BGBl. Nr. 22/1974 as amended BGBl. I Nr. 23/2020
...

6. Hauptstück—*Vorschriften für einzelne Betriebsarten*

§ 132—Betriebe mit besonderer Zweckbestimmung und Verwaltungsstellen
juristischer Personen des öffentlichen Rechts

(1) Auf Unternehmen und Betriebe, die unmittelbar politischen, koalitionspolitischen, konfessionellen, wissenschaftlichen, erzieherischen oder karitativen Zwecken dienen, ferner auf Verwaltungsstellen von juristischen Personen öffentlichen Rechts und der Österreichischen Nationalbank sind die §§ 110 bis 112 nicht anzuwenden. §§ 108 und 109 Abs. 1 und 2 sind anzuwenden, soweit nicht die besondere Zweckbestimmung betroffen ist. § 109 ist jedenfalls anzuwenden, soweit es sich um Betriebsänderungen im Sinne des § 109 Abs. 1 Z 1a, 5 und 6 handelt.
...
(4) Auf Unternehmen und Betriebe, die konfessionellen Zwecken einer gesetzlich anerkannten Kirche oder Religionsgesellschaft dienen, sind die Bestimmungen des II. Teiles nicht anzuwenden, soweit die Eigenart des Unternehmens oder des Betriebes dem entgegensteht. Jedenfalls sind die Bestimmungen über Betriebsvereinbarungen in den Angelegenheiten des § 96 Abs. 1 Z 1, 2 und 4 sowie die §§ 108 bis 112 nicht anzuwenden auf Betriebe und Verwaltungsstellen, die der Ordnung der inneren Angelegenheiten der gesetzlich anerkannten Kirchen und Religionsgesellschaften dienen, ausgenommen jedoch § 109, soweit es sich um Betriebsänderungen im Sinne des § 109 Abs. 1 Z 1a, 5 und 6 handelt.
...

Case Law

Case 1: According to the self-understanding of the IGGÖ, the training of teachers of religious instruction at the Islamic Religious Pedagogic Academy is of particular importance for achieving the denominational purpose. This Academy, therefore, is to be qualified as a 'tendency institution' within the meaning of § 132 section 4 of the ArbVG: OGH 6. 5. 1987, 14ObA29/87.

Case 2: A teacher working in the training of future Islamic religious instructors is a 'tendency bearer' within the meaning of § 132 section 4 of the ArbVG. According to this "tendency protection", the Austrian legislature leaves it to the religious societies not only in the core area directly serving denominational purposes. With regard to the denominational schools within the autonomy guaranteed in Article 15 of the StGG it is, therefore, a question of "tendency protection" whether the continued employment of a teacher is acceptable from the point of view of the religious purposes pursued by the educational institution. Since there are often connections between tendency-related and tendency-neutral reasons, the religious society in question must be free to determine the suitability of the relevant "tendency bearer" alone. Employee participation must therefore be avoided if a "tendency bearer" is affected by an employer's personal measure even if it does not refer to the tendency. It would be unreasonable for the IGGÖ not to be able independently to decide who will teach instructors at their Pedagogic Academy, but to have to deal with the reasons for the dismissal and the suitability of the teacher according to the general provisions of the Act on works constitution: OGH 28. 1. 2009, 9ObA156/08v.[5]

Case 3: The religious character of religious instruction, in this particular case Islamic, should lead to a "clear orientation of the pupils"; according to the general teaching tasks of religious instruction, religious education constitutes a "part of the personal development of the pupils." The opinion of the applicant, according to which the task of a religion instructor consisted only of a "valuation-free presentation of religious-historical facts," is not compatible with the legal tasks of religious education in Austria: OGH 16.12.2016 8ObA69/16d.

15.5 Anti-discrimination Law

In accordance with §§17 and 19 of the Equal Treatment Act 2004 (GlBG),[6] no person may be directly or indirectly discriminated against in the fields of employment and occupation[7] on the grounds of racial or ethnic origin, religion or belief, age, or sexual orientation. For the purposes of this Act, direct discrimination is taken to occur where one person is treated less favourably than another has been or would be treated in a comparable situation on any of the grounds referred to in §17 section 1 of the GlBG. Indirect discrimination is taken to occur where an apparently neutral provision, criterion or practice could have a disadvantageous effect on persons of a certain religion or belief, a certain age, or a certain sexual orientation, placing them at a particular disadvantage compared with others unless that provision, criterion or practice is

5 However, in view of the recent ECJ case law on anti-discrimination, this consistent case law of the Austrian high courts is unlikely to be upheld; cf. below fn. 9.

6 Having implemented European Directives 2000/43/EC and 2000/78/EC.

7 Additionally, a prohibition on discrimination in other areas in accordance with European Directive 2000/43/EC has been implemented on the grounds of gender and racial or ethnic origin (Part III of the GlBG).

objectively justified by a legitimate aim and the means of achieving that aim are appropriate and necessary.

In § 20 section 2 of the GlBG—adopting Directive 2000/78/EC practically word for word—§ 132 section 4 of the ArbVG has been complemented by the new anti-discrimination law providing for a specific measure for the justification of unequal treatment according to the exemption clause for occupational activities within churches and other organisations, especially to protect the ethos on which religion or belief is based. Therefore, a conjunction with the relevant legal framework as laid down in § 132 section 4 of the ArbVG is required with respect to legally recognised churches and religious societies. As far as religious denominational communities are concerned, it must be emphasised that, in contrast to the ArbVG, the anti-discrimination law makes no distinction between the different legal positions of both categories of religious community.

So far, very little case law has been developed in any of the courts. However, the Federal Equal Treatment Commission and the Ombudsman for Equal Treatment have had to deal repeatedly with cases of discrimination on religious grounds. In the overwhelming majority of cases, infringements of the Equal Treatment Act were observed and indemnities made.[8] A few disagreements concerning the wearing of Islamic headscarves (e.g. as an apprentice in a shop or a physician in a sanatorium with a conservative clientele) have also been resolved by the payment of compensation.

However, in the future, the case law of the ECJ must also be taken into account, as it has recently for the first time dealt with issues of discrimination on religious grounds, two of which concerned headscarves at a private workplace[9] and the other two are "tendency protection cases."[10]

---

8 https://www.bundeskanzleramt.gv.at/agenda/frauen-und-gleichstellung/gleichbehandlungskommissionen/gleichbehandlungskommission.html. [last accessed 16 March 2020].

9 CJEU 14. 3. 2017, Case C-57/15 Samira Achbita and Centrum voor gelijkheid van kansen en voor racismebestrijding v. G4S Secure Solutions NV and Case C-188/15 Asma Bougnaoui, Association de defense des droits de l'homme (ADDH) v. Micropole Univers SA. It should be mentioned that the judgment in the Achbita case in particular clearly leans towards the privatisation of religion and thus shows an assimilation tendency that is incompatible with the Austrian concept of law on religion.

10 The two German cases (17. 4. 2018: Case C-414/16 Vera Egenberger v Evangelisches Werk für Diakonie und Entwicklung eV; and 11. 9. 2018: Case C-68/217 [this case no. can't be right] IR v. JQ) dealt with the hiring or dismissal of employees in church institutions. Article 4(2) of Directive 2000/78/EC allows a difference of treatment if a person's religion or belief constitutes a genuine, legitimate and justified occupational requirement, having regard to the organisation's ethos. According to the Court, such measures must be subject to effective judicial review. These decisions will probably not remain without effects on the practice

Bundesgesetz über die Gleichbehandlung (Gleichbehandlungsgesetz—GlBG)
BGBl. I Nr. 66/2004 as amended BGBl. I Nr. 16/2020
…
II. Teil—*Gleichbehandlung in der Arbeitswelt ohne Unterschied der ethnischen Zugehörigkeit, der Religion oder Weltanschauung, des Alters oder der sexuellen Orientierung* (*Antidiskriminierung*)
…

§ 17—*Gleichbehandlungsgebot im Zusammenhang mit einem Arbeitsverhältnis*

(1) Auf Grund der ethnischen Zugehörigkeit, der Religion oder Weltanschauung, des Alters oder der sexuellen Orientierung darf im Zusammenhang mit einem Arbeitsverhältnis niemand unmittelbar oder mittelbar diskriminiert werden, insbesondere nicht
1. bei der Begründung des Arbeitsverhältnisses,
2. bei der Festsetzung des Entgelts,
3. bei der Gewährung freiwilliger Sozialleistungen, die kein Entgelt darstellen,
4. bei Maßnahmen der Aus- und Weiterbildung und Umschulung,
5. beim beruflichen Aufstieg, insbesondere bei Beförderungen,
6. bei den sonstigen Arbeitsbedingungen,
7. bei der Beendigung des Arbeitsverhältnisses.
(2) Abs. 1 berührt nicht die Vorschriften und die Bedingungen für die Einreise von Staatsangehörigen dritter Staaten oder staatenloser Personen oder deren Aufenthalt sowie eine Behandlung, die sich aus der Rechtsstellung von Staatsangehörigen dritter Staaten oder staatenloser Personen ergibt.

…

§ 18—*Gleichbehandlungsgebot in der sonstigen Arbeitswelt*

Aus den im § 17 genannten Gründen darf niemand unmittelbar oder mittelbar diskriminiert werden

of churches and religious societies and the 'tendency protection' case law in Austria; cf. above the case of the teacher at the Islamic Pedagogical Academy.

1. beim Zugang zur Berufsberatung, Berufsausbildung, beruflichen Weiterbildung und Umschulung außerhalb eines Arbeitsverhältnisses
2. bei der Mitgliedschaft und Mitwirkung in einer Arbeitnehmer/innen/- oder Arbeitgeber/innen/organisation oder einer Organisation, deren Mitglieder einer bestimmten Berufsgruppe angehören, einschließlich der Inanspruchnahme der Leistungen solcher Organisationen,
3. bei den Bedingungen für den Zugang zu selbstständiger Erwerbstätigkeit.

§ 19—*Begriffsbestimmungen*

(1) Eine unmittelbare Diskriminierung liegt vor, wenn eine Person auf Grund eines in § 17 genannten Grundes in einer vergleichbaren Situation eine weniger günstige Behandlung erfährt, als eine andere Person erfährt, erfahren hat oder erfahren würde.
(2) Eine mittelbare Diskriminierung liegt vor, wenn dem Anschein nach neutrale Vorschriften, Kriterien oder Verfahren Personen, die einer ethnischen Gruppe angehören, oder Personen mit einer bestimmten Religion oder Weltanschauung, eines bestimmten Alters oder mit einer bestimmten sexuellen Orientierung gegenüber anderen Personen in besonderer Weise benachteiligen können, es sei denn, die betreffenden Vorschriften, Kriterien oder Verfahren sind durch ein rechtmäßiges Ziel sachlich gerechtfertigt und die Mittel sind zur Erreichung dieses Zieles angemessen und erforderlich.
(3) Eine Diskriminierung liegt auch bei Anweisung einer Person zur Diskriminierung vor.

§ 20—*Ausnahmebestimmungen*

(1) Bei Ungleichbehandlung wegen eines Merkmals, das im Zusammenhang mit einem der in § 17 genannten Diskriminierungsgründe steht, liegt keine Diskriminierung vor, wenn das betreffende Merkmal auf Grund der Art einer bestimmten beruflichen Tätigkeit oder der Rahmenbedingungen ihrer Ausübung eine wesentliche und entscheidende berufliche Voraussetzung darstellt und sofern es sich um einen rechtmäßigen Zweck und eine angemessene Anforderung handelt.
(2) Eine Diskriminierung auf Grund der Religion oder Weltanschauung liegt in Bezug auf berufliche Tätigkeiten innerhalb von Kirchen oder anderen öffentlichen oder privaten Organisationen, deren Ethos auf religiösen Grundsätzen oder Weltanschauungen beruht, nicht vor, wenn die

Religion oder die Weltanschauung dieser Person nach der Art dieser Tätigkeiten oder der Umstände ihrer Ausübung eine wesentliche, rechtmäßige und gerechtfertigte berufliche Anforderung angesichts des Ethos der Organisation darstellt.

…

§ 21—*Belästigung*

(1) Eine Diskriminierung nach § 17 liegt auch vor, wenn eine Person
1. vom/von der Arbeitgeber/in selbst belästigt wird,
2. durch den/die Arbeitgeber/in dadurch diskriminiert wird, indem er/sie es schuldhaft unterlässt, im Falle einer Belästigung durch Dritte (Z 3) eine auf Grund gesetzlicher Bestimmungen, Normen der kollektiven Rechtsgestaltung oder des Arbeitsvertrages angemessene Abhilfe zu schaffen,
3. durch Dritte in Zusammenhang mit seinem/ihrem Arbeitsverhältnis belästigt wird oder
4. durch Dritte außerhalb eines Arbeitsverhältnisses (§ 18) belästigt wird.
(2) Belästigung liegt vor, wenn eine unerwünschte Verhaltensweise, die mit einem der Gründe nach § 17 im Zusammenhang steht, gesetzt wird,
1. die die Würde der betroffenen Person verletzt oder dies bezweckt,
2. die für die betroffene Person unerwünscht, unangebracht oder anstößig ist und
3. die ein einschüchterndes, feindseliges, entwürdigendes, beleidigendes oder demütigendes Umfeld für die betroffene Person schafft oder dies bezweckt.
(3) Eine Diskriminierung liegt auch bei Anweisung zur Belästigung einer Person vor.

[…]

§ 23—*Gebot der diskriminierungsfreien Stellenausschreibung*

Der/die Arbeitgeber/in oder private/r Arbeitsvermittler/in gemäß den §§ 4 ff. des Arbeitsmarktförderungsgesetzes, BGBl. Nr. 31/1969, oder eine mit der Arbeitsvermittlung betraute juristische Person öffentlichen Rechts darf einen Arbeitsplatz weder öffentlich noch innerhalb des Betriebes (Unternehmens) in diskriminierender Weise ausschreiben oder durch Dritte ausschreiben lassen, es sei denn, das betreffende Merkmal stellt auf Grund der Art einer bestimmten beruflichen Tätigkeit oder der Bedingungen ihrer Ausübung eine wesentliche und entscheidende berufliche Anforderung dar, sofern es sich um einen rechtmäßigen Zweck und eine angemessene Anforderung handelt.

Case Law

Courts

Case 1: The disturbance in social communication and interaction caused by the wearing of a niqab also exists in a workplace where there is contact with customers, employees and the employer. Therefore, the face not being veiled is an essential and decisive professional prerequisite due to the nature of the activities carried out in a notary's office: OGH 25.05.2016, 9ObA117/15v.

Equal Treatment Commission[11]

Case 1: The avoidance of specific, serious occupational accident risks by means of appropriate clothing regulations does not represent a particular disadvantage for Muslim women by reason of the employer's obligations arising out of the Employee Protection Act, if safety considerations for working on dangerous machines[12] are appropriate to justify the measures in question. A condition for this is that the prohibition also refers to the wearing of clothing or jewellery that is comparable with regard to the risk potential and exclusively considered from the perspective of employee protection: GBK II/27/07.

Case 2: In the medical field in particular, the right to wear a headscarf in the workplace as an expression of one's own religious belief is in line with the existing requirements with regard to aspects of hygiene and patient safety: GBK II/70/08.

Case 3: The general exclusion of certain groups of people—such as 'women with a headscarf'—formulated as an applicant's request in the application procedure is prohibited as an instruction to discriminate and is subject to compensation: GBK II/31/07; GBK II/70/08.

Case 4: Demanding that an employee not wear the headscarf during an internship in a bakery or even to take it off some way before entering the shop is direct discrimination based on religion and ethnicity: GBK II/79/09.

11 The Equal Treatment Commission (*Gleichbehandlungskommission—GBK*) hears arbitration proceedings in accordance with Article 7(1) of Directive 2000/43/EC resp. [Article 9(1) of Directive 2000/78/EC. The procedure serves to mediate between employers and employees prior to adjudication. The decisions of the *GBK* can end with a proposal for compensation and the implementation of operational measures to avoid discrimination and are published anonymously.

12 In the case in question it was a job as a laundry assistant in an automated industrial laundry.

15.6 Religious Holidays and Free Time to Fulfil Religious Duties

In line with the historical background, most of the holidays recognised by the state and protected by law as days of rest from work (settled in the Act on Rest from Work 1983—ARG) are Christian or, more precisely, Catholic holidays; only two holidays (1 May and 26 October) are secular. Since the middle of the last century several administrative decrees, circulars and similar announcements or collective labour agreements have already considered the specific holidays of religious minorities. Meanwhile, efforts are generally being made to remedy the situation at the level of collective labour agreements and administrative decrees.

According to § 8 section 1 of the ARG, employees who work at weekends or during holiday periods have a legal claim to time off work on the grounds that it is necessary for them to fulfil their religious obligations unless it is possible for them to do so outside normal working hours and if the exemption is compatible with the operating requirements of the business or enterprise.

In §§ 13 and 20 of the IslamG 2015,[13] certain Muslim and Alevite holidays (including prayer-times on Fridays or Thursdays, respectively) are mentioned, although without direct consequences in the field of labour law as clarified in the explanatory notes to the bill. However, disturbing and avoidable disruption surrounding places of worship has to be avoided.

The additional holiday in Austria for evangelical Christians and Old Catholics on Good Friday was considered discriminatory by the ECJ.[14] In implementing the ECJ decision, the Austrian legislature introduced the chance to determine a 'personal holiday' for everyone, which, however, is counted as a vacation day. This "personal holiday" enables members of all religious communities to celebrate a holiday in accordance with their religious rules.

Bundesgesetz vom 3. Feber 1983 über die wöchentliche Ruhezeit und die Arbeitsruhe an Feiertagen (Arbeitsruhegesetz—ARG), BGBl. Nr. 144/1983 as amended BGBl. I Nr. 22/2019

...

§ 7a—*Einseitiger Urlaubsantritt („persönlicher Feiertag“)*

(1) Der Arbeitnehmer kann den Zeitpunkt des Antritts eines Tages des ihm zustehenden Urlaubs einmal pro Urlaubsjahr einseitig bestimmen.

13 See chapter 3.

14 CJEU 22. 1. 2019, C-193/17 Cresco Investigation GmbH vs. Markus Achatzi.

Der Arbeitnehmer hat den Zeitpunkt spätestens drei Monate im Vorhinein schriftlich bekannt zu geben.
(2) Es steht dem Arbeitnehmer frei, auf Ersuchen des Arbeitgebers den bekannt gegebenen Urlaubstag nicht anzutreten. In diesem Fall hat der Arbeitnehmer weiterhin Anspruch auf diesen Urlaubstag. Weiters hat er für den bekannt gegebenen Tag außer dem Urlaubsentgelt Anspruch auf das für die geleistete Arbeit gebührende Entgelt, insgesamt daher das doppelte Entgelt, womit das Recht gemäß Abs. 1 erster Satz konsumiert ist.
(3) …

§ 8—*Freizeit zur Erfüllung der religiösen Pflichten*

(1) Der Arbeitnehmer, der während der Wochenend- oder Feiertagsruhe beschäftigt wird, hat auf Verlangen Anspruch auf die zur Erfüllung seiner religiösen Pflichten notwendige Freizeit, wenn diese Pflichten nicht außerhalb der Arbeitszeit erfüllt werden können und die Freistellung von der Arbeit mit den Erfordernissen des Betriebes vereinbar ist.
(2) Der Arbeitnehmer hat diesen Anspruch bei Vereinbarung der Wochenend- oder Feiertagsarbeit, spätestens jedoch zwei Tage vorher, bei späterer Vereinbarung sofort, dem Arbeitgeber gegenüber geltend zu machen.

Case Law

Case 1: A Muslim employee had been dismissed for worshipping daily in the presence of other employees, using a carpet and other religious objects. He was also accused of leaving the business before closing time in order to go to the mosque on Friday afternoon, without taking working instructions into consideration. The Court stated that such behaviour disturbed the planned distribution of labour and irritated co-workers who also held the same fundamental right to religious freedom (in its negative dimension). § 8 of the ARG stipulates that the free time required to carry out religious duties must be granted if the time off from work is compatible with the requirements of the company: OGH 27. 3. 1996, 9ObA18/96.

15.7 Social Law

The Islamic religious communities and their institutions are fully integrated in the general obligatory social insurance scheme as laid down in § 4 of the

General Social Insurance Act (ASVG)[15] covering health, accident and retirement pension insurance. There is special provision only for priests as well as members of religious orders and similar institutions of the Catholic Church, which are exempt from full insurance liability (§ 7 section 1 no. 7).

Bundesgesetz vom 9. September 1955 über die Allgemeine Sozialversicherung (Allgemeines Sozialversicherungsgesetz—ASVG)
BGBl. Nr. 189/1955 as amended BGBl. I Nr. 23/2020
…
VIERTER TEIL—*Pensionsversicherung*

ABSCHNITT III—*Pensionsversicherung der Angestellten*

…
§ 271—*Berufsunfähigkeitspension*

(1) Anspruch auf Berufsunfähigkeitspension hat der (die) Versicherte, wenn
1. die Berufsunfähigkeit (§ 273) voraussichtlich sechs Monate andauert oder andauern würde,
2. die Wartezeit erfüllt ist (§ 236) und
3. er (sie) am Stichtag (§ 223 Abs. 2) noch nicht die Voraussetzungen für eine Alterspension nach diesem oder einem anderen Bundesgesetz, mit Ausnahme der Alterspension nach § 4 Abs. 2 APG, erfüllt hat.
…

§ 273—*Begriff der Berufsunfähigkeit*

(1) Als berufsunfähig gilt der Versicherte, dessen Arbeitsfähigkeit infolge seines körperlichen oder geistigen Zustandes auf weniger als die Hälfte derjenigen eines körperlich und geistig gesunden Versicherten von ähnlicher Ausbildung und gleichwertigen Kenntnissen und Fähigkeiten herabgesunken ist.

Case Law

Case 1: The benefits of a disability pension presuppose that the insured person can no longer pursue a profession in his or her professional group due to his

15 BGBl. Nr. 189/1955 as amended BGBl. I Nr. 23/2020.

or her mental or physical condition. The starting point is the profession that the insured practised recently. This occupation determines the occupational group in which a similar education and equivalent knowledge and skills are required. Considering the training of Islamic prayer leaders, content-related activity is possible in all activities related to the administrative management of a mosque, such as archive and library administration. It would also be reasonable to undergo additional training or specialisation in the previous occupation in order to create the prerequisites for employability in the labour market. For a prayer leader who attended a three- to four-year Qur'anic school, six months of additional training would be required for him to undertake the tasks of a teacher of Islamic religious instruction. There is, therefore, no obstacle to referral for an Islamic prayer leader that would entail the granting of a disability pension: OGH 8. 5. 2001, 10ObS12/01i.

CHAPTER 16

Islamic Slaughter and Dietary Rules

16.1 Islamic Ritual Slaughter

In accordance with §§12 and 19 of the IslamG,[1] the Islamic Religious Society has the right to organise the production of meat products and other food in accordance with its internal regulations. At the end of the nineteenth century in Austria, as elsewhere in Europe, discussions began about Jewish ritual slaughter in connection with animal protection.[2] At the end of the twentieth century, these discussions flared up again primarily in connection with Islamic slaughter.

Originally, the competence for animal protection law fell within the sphere of competence of the *Bundesländer*, entailing diverging regulations with regard to ritual slaughter, partly in contrast to the constitutional guarantees. In 2004, after an extensive and quite emotionally charged public debate, a new Federal Act on Animal Protection (TSchG)[3] was enacted, establishing a uniform legal situation throughout the whole of federal territory.[4] According to this law, slaughter without prior stunning is in principle forbidden. As regards 'compulsory religious precepts or bans of legally recognised churches and religious societies' which contravene this rule, ritual slaughter may be deemed lawful by administrative approval if it complies with certain detailed prerequisites concerning the slaughtering procedure.[5] In any case, stunning must be carried out immediately after the act of incision and in such a manner that the animal does not suffer unnecessary pain, harm and fear. As a consequence, ritual slaughter

1 See chapter 3.

2 See Potz, Richard, "Historische Einleitung", in Potz Richard, Schinkele, Brigitte, and Wieshaider, Wolfgang (eds.), *Schächten. Religionsfreiheit und Tierschutz* (Freistadt: Plöchl, 2001), pp. 27–48.

3 BGBl. I Nr. 118/2004 as amended BGBl. I Nr. 86/2018.

4 Cf. Potz, Richard, and Schinkele, Brigitte, *Religionsrecht im Überblick* (Vienna: facultas.wuv, 2nd ed., pp. 86 ff.; Wieshaider, Wolfgang, "Iterum: Schächten: Rund ums neue österreichische Tierschutzgesetz," in *Österreichisches Archiv für Recht und Religion*, vol. 52 (2005), pp. 227–262.

5 Cf. Recital no. 6 of Council Directive 93/119/EC of 22 December 1993 on the protection of animals at the time of slaughter or killing, which stipulates that member states in favour of religious rites can provide exemptions from the obligation to stun before slaughtering. Austria has made use of this possibility.

does not commit the offence of cruelty to animals in accordance with § 222 of the StGB, which is an offence committed by a person who cruelly mistreats or inflicts unnecessary torture on an animal.

If the aforementioned points of criticism are taken into consideration, this act is essentially in conformity with the Constitutional Court's and the Supreme Court's decision-making from the perspective of constitutional as well as criminal law.[6] Accordingly, religious slaughter neither offends public morals nor infringes public order.

Bundesgesetz über den Schutz der Tiere (Tierschutzgesetz—TSchG)
BGBl. I Nr. 118/2004 as amended BGBl. I Nr. 86/2018

1. Hauptstück—*Allgemeine Bestimmungen*

§ 1—*Zielsetzung*

Ziel dieses Bundesgesetzes ist der Schutz des Lebens und des Wohlbefindens der Tiere aus der besonderen Verantwortung des Menschen für das Tier als Mitgeschöpf.

…

§ 4—*Begriffsbestimmungen*

Die nachstehenden Begriffe haben in diesem Bundesgesetz jeweils folgende Bedeutung:

…

13. Schlachten: das Töten eines Tieres durch Blutentzug und nachfolgende Ausweidung zum Zweck der Fleischgewinnung

…

§ 5—*Verbot der Tierquälerei*

(1) Es ist verboten, einem Tier ungerechtfertigt Schmerzen, Leiden oder Schäden zuzufügen oder es in schwere Angst zu versetzen.

…

6 VfGH 17. 12. 1998, B3028/1997, VfSlg. 15394/1998; OGH 28. 3. 1996, 15 Os 27/96 a.o.; VwGH 30. 4. 1897, B. 2468, VwSlg. 10666/1897; 248 A/1907. Cf. Potz, Richard, Schinkele, Brigitte, and Wieshaider, Wolfgang (eds.) (fn. 176).

§ 6—*Verbot der Tötung*

(1) Es ist verboten, Tiere ohne vernünftigen Grund zu töten.
…

2. Abschnitt—*Besondere Bestimmungen*
…

§ 32—*Schlachtung oder Tötung*

(1) Unbeschadet des Verbotes der Tötung nach § 6 darf die Tötung eines Tieres nur so erfolgen, dass jedes ungerechtfertigte Zufügen von Schmerzen, Leiden, Schäden oder schwerer Angst vermieden wird.
(2) Die Schlachtung, Tötung, Verbringung, Unterbringung, Ruhigstellung, Betäubung und Entblutung eines Tieres darf nur durch Personen vorgenommen werden, die dazu die notwendigen Kenntnisse und Fähigkeiten besitzen.
(3) Das Schlachten von Tieren ohne Betäubung vor dem Blutentzug ist verboten. Ist eine Betäubung unter den gegebenen Umständen, wie etwa bei einer Notschlachtung, nicht möglich oder stehen ihr zwingende religiöse Gebote oder Verbote einer gesetzlich anerkannten Religionsgemeinschaft entgegen (rituelle Schlachtung), so ist die Schlachtung so vorzunehmen, dass dem Tier nicht unnötig Schmerzen, Leiden, Schäden oder schwere Angst zugefügt werden.
(4) Rituelle Schlachtungen dürfen nur in einer dafür eingerichteten und von der Behörde dafür zugelassenen Schlachtanlage durchgeführt werden.
(5) Rituelle Schlachtungen ohne vorausgehende Betäubung der Schlachttiere dürfen nur vorgenommen werden, wenn dies auf Grund zwingender religiöser Gebote oder Verbote einer gesetzlich anerkannten Religionsgemeinschaft notwendig ist und die Behörde eine Bewilligung zur Schlachtung ohne Betäubung erteilt hat. Die Behörde hat die Bewilligung zur Durchführung der rituellen Schlachtung nur dann zu erteilen, wenn sichergestellt ist, dass
1. die rituellen Schlachtungen von Personen vorgenommen werden, die über die dazu notwendigen Kenntnisse und Fähigkeiten verfügen,
2. die rituellen Schlachtungen ausschließlich in Anwesenheit eines mit der Schlachttier- und Fleischuntersuchung beauftragten Tierarztes erfolgen,
3. Einrichtungen vorhanden sind, die gewährleisten, dass die für die ritu-

elle Schlachtung vorgesehenen Tiere so rasch wie möglich in eine für die Schlachtung notwendige Position gebracht werden können,
4. die Schlachtung so erfolgt, dass die großen Blutgefäße im Halsbereich mit einem Schnitt eröffnet werden,
5. die Tiere unmittelbar nach dem Eröffnen der Blutgefäße wirksam betäubt werden,
6. sofort nach dem Schnitt die Betäubung wirksam wird und
7. die zur rituellen Schlachtung bestimmten Tiere erst dann in die dafür vorgesehene Position gebracht werden, wenn der Betäuber zur Vornahme der Betäubung bereit ist.
(6) Der Bundesminister für Gesundheit, Familie und Jugend hat entsprechend dem anerkannten Stand der wissenschaftlichen Erkenntnisse durch Verordnung nähere Vorschriften über das Töten oder Schlachten von Tieren zu erlassen. Er kann bestimmte Tötungs- oder Schlachtmethoden verbieten, von einer Bewilligung abhängig machen, zulassen oder gebieten. Er hat insbesondere Regelungen über
1. die Anforderungen an Schlachthöfe,
2. das Verbringen und Unterbringen von Tieren in Schlachthöfen
3. das Ruhigstellen der Tiere vor dem Betäuben, Schlachten oder Töten,
4. das Betäuben, Schlachten und Töten von Tieren,
5. das Entbluten von Tieren,
6. das Schlachten oder Töten außerhalb von Schlachthöfen im Einvernehmen mit dem Bundesminister für Land- und Forstwirtschaft, Umwelt und Wasserwirtschaft,
7. die Anforderungen an Schlachtstätten, in denen rituelle Schlachtungen durchgeführt werden,
...
zu treffen.

Case Law

Case 1: Slaughtering anaesthetised animals in accordance with Jewish and Islamic religious provisions is not cruelty to animals within the meaning of § 222 section 1 of the Criminal Code. The ritual slaughter of sheep is done in a socially adequate manner that excludes illegality. Since this absence of illegality is a negative element of the offence of cruelty to animals, the slaughter of animals according to the religious regulations of Muslims and Jews cannot constitute the above offence (cf. VwSlg 10.666/1897; VwSlg 5248A/1907): VfSlg 15394/1998.

16.2 Islamic Dietary Rules

In accordance with §§12 section 2 and 19 section 2 of the IslamG,[7] with regard to meals for members of the Religious Society in the army, in prison, in public hospitals, nursing, care or similar institutions, as well as in public schools, the internal dietary regulations must be respected.

16.2.1 *Islamic Meals in the Army*

In order to facilitate compliance with the religious obligations (prayer, fasting, etc.), the so-called 'strict faith-certificate' is issued on the basis of an agreement with the IGGÖ.[8] Deeply religious members of the IGGÖ (membership has to be proved during medical examination by supplying a confirmation of the 'Oberster Rat der Islamischen Glaubensgemeinschaft in Österreich') may be conscripted into special bodies of troops in order to ensure the fulfilment of their religious needs.

If strict faith is claimed after conscription into a specific body of troops, the following rule applies:

- If the recruiting body is able to satisfy religious expectations without causing disturbance to the ordinary running of the troop, the affected soldier may stay with it.
- If this is not possible, the military command may organise a transfer to a special body of troops in accordance with the capacity available and the date of enlistment.

16.2.2 *Islamic Meals in Prison*

Bundesgesetz vom 26. März 1969 über den Vollzug der Freiheitsstrafen und der mit Freiheitsentziehung verbundenen vorbeugenden Maßnahmen (Strafvollzugsgesetz—StVG)
BGBl. Nr. 144/169 as amended BGBl. I Nr. 100/2018

…

Zweiter Unterabschnitt—*Verpflegung, Bekleidung und Unterbringung*

---

7 See chapter 3.

8 Bundesminister für Landesverteidigung BMLV (ed.), *Soldat. Leitfaden für den Dienst im Bundesheer* (Wolkersdorf, 2019).

§ 38—*Verpflegung*

(1) Die Strafgefangenen sind mit einfacher Anstaltskost ausreichend zu verpflegen. Die Kost muß den ernährungswissenschaftlichen Erkenntnissen entsprechen und schmackhaft sein; sie ist zu den für die Einnahme von Mahlzeiten allgemein üblichen Tageszeiten auszugeben.
(2) Bei der Verpflegung ist auf eine reichlichere Kost für Strafgefangene, die Arbeit verrichten, auf Abweichungen von der allgemeinen Kost, die der Anstaltsarzt für einzelne Strafgefangene wegen ihres Gesundheitszustandes verordnet, sowie auf die dem Glaubensbekenntnis der Strafgefangenen entsprechenden Speisegebote Rücksicht zu nehmen; ist eine Rücksichtnahme auf diese Speisegebote nach den Einrichtungen der Anstalt nicht möglich, so ist den Strafgefangenen zu gestatten, sich insoweit eine diesen Geboten entsprechende Verpflegung unter Bedachtnahme auf Art und Maß der Anstaltskost von dritter Seite zur Verfügung stellen zu lassen.

CHAPTER 17

Islamic Dress

In Austria, where there were traditionally no problems with Islamic clothing, discussions about the admissibility of religiously motivated clothing, especially the different forms of Islamic headscarf and veil, have significantly increased in recent years. This became especially clear when the Anti-Face-Covering Act (*Bundesgesetz über das Verbot der Verhüllung des Gesichts in der Öffentlichkeit—AGesVG*) was adopted in the context of a bundle of new laws and amendments regarding integration.[1]

In parallel some contextual regulations concerning headscarves and veils were enacted, especially as regards schoolchildren. Moreover 'headscarf cases' are dominating the decisions of the Federal Equal Treatment Commission regarding discrimination on the grounds of religion and belief.[2]

17.1 Kindergarten and School

In 2018, a headscarf ban for kindergartens was introduced.[3] The explanatory notes to the bill point out that wearing a headscarf before sexual maturity is not mandatory in Islam and, beyond that, justify the provision as follows: '[w]earing the Islamic headscarf by children in elementary educational institutions can lead to early sexual segregation, which is not compatible with the fundamental Austrian values and social norms. The orientation towards religious values must not conflict with the goals of civic education, which are based on the fundamental values, which should also ensure equality between men and women.'

The wearing of a headscarf by Muslim girls as religiously based clothing in the school sector was expressly approved as falling under the protection of religious freedom until 2019.[4] In that year a 'headscarf ban' for primary school children was introduced through an amendment to the School Teaching Act. This measure was justified by the fact that it 'serves the social integration of

---

1 See chapter 8.

2 See chapter 15.

3 Article III Abs. 1 *Vereinbarung gemäß Article 15a B-VG zwischen dem Bund und den Ländern über die Elementarpädagogik für die Kindergartenjahre 2018/19 bis 2021/22*, BGBl. I Nr. 103/2018.

4 Erlass des Bildungsministeriums vom 23. Juni 2004, Zl. 20.251/3-III/3/2004.

children in accordance with local customs, the preservation of the constitutional basic values and educational goals of the Federal Constitution and the equality of men and women' (§ 43a).[5] The latest government programme has announced that the existing headscarf ban should be extended to schoolchildren up to the age of 14, when religious maturity is reached.[6]

Schulunterrichtsgesetz

BGBl. Nr. 472/1986 as amended BGBl. I Nr. 23/2020

…

§ 43a

(1) Um die bestmögliche Entwicklung und Entfaltung aller Schülerinnen und Schüler sicherzustellen, ist diesen bis zum Ende des Schuljahres, in welchem sie das 10. Lebensjahr vollenden, das Tragen weltanschaulich oder religiös geprägter Bekleidung mit der eine Verhüllung des Hauptes verbunden ist, untersagt. Dies dient der sozialen Integration von Kindern gemäß den lokalen Gebräuchen und Sitten, der Wahrung der verfassungsrechtlichen Grundwerte und Bildungsziele der Bundesverfassung sowie der Gleichstellung von Mann und Frau.
(2) Bei Verstoß gegen das Verbot gemäß Abs. 1 hat die Schulleiterin bzw. der Schulleiter unverzüglich die jeweils zuständige Bildungsdirektion zu verständigen. Diese hat die Erziehungsberechtigten unverzüglich, jedenfalls innerhalb von 4 Schultagen, zu einem verpflichtenden Gespräch zu laden. In dem Gespräch sind die Gründe für den Verstoß zu erörtern. Zur Vermeidung weiterer Verstöße sind die Erziehungsberechtigten über ihre Verantwortung aufzuklären; dies ist schriftlich festzuhalten und der Schulleiterin bzw. dem Schulleiter zur Kenntnis zu bringen.
(3) Findet nach dem Gespräch ein weiterer Verstoß gegen das Verbot gemäß Abs. 1 statt, oder kommen die Erziehungsberechtigten der ver-

5 NR GP XXVI, 612: https://www.parlament.gv.at/PAKT/VHG/XXVI/I/I_00612/fname_751626.pdf, p. 3.

6 Cf. Österreichische Volkspartei and Die Grünen—Die Grüne Alternative (eds.), *Aus Verantwortung für Österreich, Regierungsprogramm 2020–2024*, https://www.wienerzeitung.at/_em_daten/_wzo/2020/01/02/200102-1510_regierungsprogramm_2020_gesamt.pdf, p. 207 [last accessed 8 April 2020].

pflichtenden Ladung nach nochmaliger Aufforderung nicht nach, so stellt dieser eine Verwaltungsübertretung durch die Erziehungsberechtigten dar und ist von der Bezirksverwaltungsbehörde mit einer Geldstrafe bis zu 440 €, im Fall der Uneinbringlichkeit mit Ersatzfreiheitsstrafe bis zu zwei Wochen zu bestrafen.

17.2 Islamic Dress in Hospitals

As a rule, the wearing of a headscarf is permitted in hospitals if, in particular, patient safety and patient rights, employee protection, hygienic regulations and work clothing regulations are not violated. As an example, the relevant decree of the Vienna Medical Association should be mentioned.

Erlass zum „Tragen von Kopfbedeckungen im Arbeitskontext" an alle Dienststellen der Unternehmung Krankenanstaltenverbund,

GED-104/2006/BGD, October 18th 2006

Der Wiener Krankenanstaltenverbund (KAV) ist ein multikulturelles Unternehmen. Ein beachtlicher Teil der in den Krankenhäusern und Geriatriezentren des KAV betreuten PatientInnen sowie deren Angehörige haben einen multikulturellen Hintergrund. Diese werden während ihres Aufenthaltes in unseren Einrichtungen zu einem ebenfalls beachtlichen Teil von fachlich hoch qualifizierten MitarbeiterInnen mit ebenfalls multikulturellen Kompetenzen betreut.
Grundlegende Bedeutung kommt in diesem Zusammenhang folgendem Leitsatz der Unternehmung KAV zu, welcher gleichermaßen für PatientInnen als auch für MitarbeiterInnen gilt: „Grundlage unseres Handelns ist die Achtung aller Menschen ohne Rücksicht auf Herkunft, Religion, Alter und Rasse."
Aus diesem Grundsatz heraus wird folgende Positionierung der Führung des KAV im Bezug auf das Tragen von Kopfbedeckungen im Arbeitskontext des KAV bekannt gegeben, der zu folgen allen MitarbeiterInnen und insbesondere allen Führungskräften mit Nachdruck nahe gelegt wird.
Das Tragen einer Kopfbedeckung als Ausdruck gelebter Religiosität und Teil der Glaubenspraxis bringt das individuelle Bekenntnis der/des Tragenden zum Ausdruck. Dieses Bekenntnis ist zu respektieren und das Tragen zu ermöglichen, wenn folgende maßgebliche Grundsätze nicht verletzt werden:

Die PatientInnen-Sicherheit und die PatientInnen-Rechte, der ArbeitnehmerInnen-Schutz, die hygienischen Vorschriften sowie die Dienstbekleidungsvorschriften.
Nachstehende Beispiele werden ohne Anspruch auf Vollständigkeit und unter Hinweis auf die geltenden Bekleidungsvorschriften angeführt: Operationsbereiche bzw. OP-ähnliche Einheiten, Dialyse-Einheiten, Isoliereinheiten mit festgelegter Schutzbekleidung, Intensiv- und vergleichbare Einheiten bzw. Aufwach- und Überwachungseinheiten und psychiatrische Einrichtungen.
Die Entscheidung und Verantwortung zur Umsetzung dieser Feststellungen obliegt den jeweiligen Führungskräften vor Ort. Entstehende Fragen und Diskussionen sind in partnerschaftlich wertschätzender Art und Weise zu klären bzw. zu führen. Die Direktion des KAV wird in weiterer Folge Informationsangebote bereitstellen. Zudem stehen zur Unterstützung und Klärung offener Fragen die Stabsstelle Recht in der Generaldirektion sowie für das Allgemeine Krankenhaus und Universitätskliniken die dortige Rechtsabteilung in der Direktion zur Verfügung.
Abschließend wird hier ergänzend betont, dass jede politisch und weltanschaulich geprägte Manifestation im Dienstbereich und im örtlichen Zusammenhang der Dienstverrichtung sowie in den Dienststellen des KAV nicht gestattet ist und somit zu unterbleiben hat.
...

17.3 The Islamic Veil in the Courtroom

During a trial by jury concerning membership of a terrorist association in accordance with § 278b section 2 of the Criminal Code (StGB), the defendant refused to take off her *niqab*. This was classified as 'unseemly behaviour' which interfered with the order of judicial proceedings, and the woman, therefore, was excluded from attending the proceedings pursuant to § 234 of the Code of Criminal Procedure (StPO).

Strafprozessordnung 1975 (StPO),
BGBl. Nr. 631/1975 (WV) as amended BGBl. I Nr. 24/2020
...

§ 234

Wenn der Angeklagte die Ordnung der Verhandlung durch ungeziemendes Benehmen stört und ungeachtet der Ermahnung des Vorsitzenden und der Androhung, dass er aus der Sitzung werde entfernt werden, nicht davon absteht, so kann er durch Beschluss des Schöffengerichts auf einige Zeit oder für die ganze Dauer der Verhandlung aus dieser entfernt, die Sitzung in seiner Abwesenheit fortgesetzt und ihm das Urteil durch ein Mitglied des Schöffengerichts in Gegenwart des Schriftführers verkündet werden.
…

Case Law

Case 1: Because having one's face uncovered is considered an uncontested fundamental principle of common human communication in Austria, it was the defendant's task to explain convincingly why her behaviour towards the Court could be considered to be religiously motivated, and not a political and ideological demonstration for which a Courtroom was certainly not the right place. The Supreme Court took the view that the defendant had failed to allay these doubts and to show clearly her respect for the dignity of the Court: OGH 27. 8. 2008, 13Os83/08t; OGH 27. 8. 2009, 13Os 9/09y.[7]

17.4 Headscarves on Passport Photos

The wearing of a headscarf for religious reasons in passport photos is permitted.

Verordnung der Bundesministerin für Inneres über die Durchführung des Passgesetzes (Passgesetz-Durchführungsverordnung—PassG-DV)
BGBl. II Nr. 223/2006 as amended 209/2018
…

7 See Schinkele, Brigitte, "Verschleierung einer Angeklagten im Gerichtssaal? Überlegungen aus grundrechtlicher Sicht," in Bunzl, John, and Hafez, Farid (eds.) (fn. 111), pp. 156–167.

§ 4—*Lichtbild*

…

(4) Der Kopf der Person soll etwa 2/3 des Bildes einnehmen. Der Augenabstand muss zumindest 8 Millimeter betragen. Das Lichtbild muss die Person in einer Frontalaufnahme, mit unverdeckten Augen und neutralem Gesichtsausdruck zeigen, die Hauttöne sind möglichst natürlich wiederzugeben. Eine Darstellung der Person mit geneigtem oder gedrehtem Kopf ist unzulässig. Das Tragen von Kopfbedeckungen ist nur aus medizinischen oder religiösen Gründen zulässig.

CHAPTER 18

Family Law

Matrimonial and family law are fields in which religious legal systems have a great many regulations, resulting in the people having widespread legal awareness and deep cultural conditioning. This is the reason why Muslims try to solve family conflicts within the community and, therefore, normally have reservations about bringing them before Austrian courts or involving other public authorities.[1]

18.1 Matrimonial Law

Until 1938 marriage law in accordance with the Civil Code of 1811 (*Allgemeines Bürgerliches Gesetzbuch*—ABGB) was characterised by a religiously determined legal pluralism with different regulations for Catholics, other Christians (Protestants and Orthodox) and Jews. It is interesting that on the occasion of the legal recognition of Islam in 1912 the inclusion of Islamic family law in the ABGB was discussed but finally rejected.[2] Austrian matrimonial law has lost its religious orientation with the "Act for the unification of the law of marriage and divorce in the Country of Austria and the Rest of the Territory of the Reich" (*Ehegesetz*—EheG) from 6 July 1938.[3] Since then, religious marriages have had no civil consequences; they merely represent an act of public manifestation of one's religion.

Since the last third of the twentieth Century in Austria as well as in practically all European countries family law reforms have been carried out, and have tended to widen the gap with Islamic law. The main objectives of this legis-

1 Cf. in particular Schmied, Martina, *Familienkonflikte zwischen Scharia und Bürgerlichem Recht. Konfliktlösungsmodell im Vorfeld der Justiz am Beispiel Österreichs* (Frankfurt/Main-Vienna: Peter Lang, 1999).

2 The Austro-Hungarian ministry responsible for the administration of Bosnia and Herzegovina in its opinion for the preparatory commission was in favour of inserting the principles of Islamic marriage law in the ABGB—at least as regards impediments and separation—which were acceptable from the standpoint of Austrian state legislation (cf. Potz, Richard, fn. 1, p. 400).

3 dRGBl. I S 807/1938 as amended BGBl. I Nr. 59/2017. After 1945 the EheG was transferred to the legal system of the Austrian Republic except for provisions containing ideological traits of National-Socialism.

lation were to replace the traditional patriarchal family model with an equal partnership between the spouses, equal treatment of legitimate and illegitimate children, facilitating adoptions, and the expansion of matrimonial law to include same-sex partnerships.

In accordance with § 582 section 2 of the Code of Civil Procedure (*Zivilprozessordnung*—ZPO[4]) family law is exempt from arbitration. Therefore, decisions by religious courts cannot have civil law consequences in matters of family law, unless those decisions are of foreign courts and governed by the rules of private international law.[5]

Austrian marriage law includes the prohibition of bigamy and polygamy, which are incompatible with the basic values of Austrian law.[6] Moreover, bigamy is a criminal offence pursuant to § 192 Criminal Code. In Austria, for members of a state where Islamic law is applied, pursuant to § 6 of the Act on Private International Law (*Internationales Privatrechts-Gesetz*—IPRG),[7] marrying for a second time with a member of the same or another state which has an Islamic family law is forbidden. As long as there is no sufficient domestic relationship in Austria, a man living with two wives is not a violation of the *ordre public*. In the area of family reunification, however, the *ordre public* of the law of aliens is relevant. In accordance with § 2 section 1 no. 9 of the Act on Settlement and Residence (*Niederlassungs- und Aufenthaltsgesetz*—NAG)[8] the other spouses are not family members entitled to obtain residence permits, if in the case of a multiple marriage a spouse is already living in the federal territory.

Gesetz zur Vereinheitlichung des Rechts der Eheschließung und der Ehescheidung im Lande Österreich vom 6. Juli 1938 (Ehegesetz—EheG) dRGBl. I S 807/1938 as amended BGBl. I Nr. 59/2017

4 RGBl. Nr. 113/1895 as amended BGBl. I Nr. 109/2018.

5 See chapter 18.3.

6 Given the experience of the Austrian authorities with polygamy, it is remarkable that a systematic guide to the "Matrimonial law, family law and inheritance of the Muslims of the Hanafite rite," published 1883 to monitor the administration of justice in Islamic courts, explicitly recognised the institution of polygamy for Bosnia.

7 Bundesgesetz über das internationale Privatrecht, BGBl. Nr. 304/1978 as amended BGBl. I Nr. 72/2019, see chapter 18.3.

8 See chapter 7.

§ 1—*Ehefähigkeit*

(1) Ehefähig ist, wer volljährig und entscheidungsfähig ist.
(2) Das Gericht hat eine Person, die das 16. Lebensjahr vollendet hat, auf ihren Antrag für ehefähig zu erklären, wenn der künftige Ehegatte volljährig ist und sie für diese Ehe reif erscheint; die minderjährige Person bedarf zur Eingehung der Ehe der Zustimmung des gesetzlichen Vertreters. Verweigert dieser die Zustimmung, so hat das Gericht sie auf Antrag der minderjährigen Person, die ihrer bedarf, zu ersetzen, wenn keine gerechtfertigten Gründe für die Weigerung vorliegen.

…
§ 8—*Doppelehe*

Niemand darf eine Ehe eingehen, bevor seine frühere Ehe für nichtig erklärt oder aufgelöst worden ist.

…
§ 24—*Doppelehe*

Eine Ehe ist nichtig, wenn ein Teil zur Zeit ihrer Schließung mit einer dritten Person in gültiger Ehe oder eingetragener Partnerschaft lebte.

Case Law
Case 1: Monogamy and the prohibition of multiple marriages (bigamy) belong to the indispensable basic values that shape the Austrian legal system: VfGH 11. 10. 2012, B 99/12; VwGH 6. 9. 2018, Ra 2018/18/0094.[9]

18.2 Parent and Child Law

As far as is possible and feasible, both parents should take care of a child by mutual agreement. In all matters concerning a minor child, in particular custody and personal contacts, the child's wellbeing must be taken as the guiding principle and shall be guaranteed as best as possible. Third parties may interfere with parental rights only to the extent that they are permitted to do so by the parents themselves, directly by law or by an official order. Official interven-

9 Cf. below the case law on § 6 IPRG.

tions in parental rights include the withdrawal and limitation of custody. Such measures may be taken only if the child's wellbeing is at risk.

If the parents' marriage or the domestic community is dissolved, the custody of both parents remains intact. They may, however, conclude an agreement in court whereby one parent alone has custody.

The family law reforms of recent decades have improved and revised the regulations regarding custody and the use of foster parents to achieve the best interests of the child (§§158ff. of the ABGB new version).

Children enjoy freedom of religion or belief. Until minors have reached religious maturity, their parents or legal guardians have to act on their behalf in religious matters. Full legal capacity is reached with the completion of the 18th year of life, while religious maturity is reached as early as at the age of 14. From the age of 12 upwards, the religious confession of a child cannot be changed against its will.[10] At the same time, parents can exercise their own individual right to bring up and educate their children, as part of their fundamental rights of religious freedom and of respect for private and family life. As long as the marriage exists, no spouse may decide without the other's consent that a child should be raised in a confession other than that which was the common confession at the time of marriage, or in a confession other than previously, or that the child should be withdrawn from religious instruction at school.

Islamic religious societies and their members are authorised to guide their children and young people through all traditional customs and to educate them in accordance with their religious doctrine (§11 section 4 of the IslamG). The explanatory notes to the bill explicitly point out that circumcision according to the Islamic tradition is covered by this provision. In accordance with §90 section 3 of the Criminal Law Code consent to genital mutilation or any other genital injury which causes a lasting impairment of sexual sensation is inadmissible.[11]

Allgemeines bürgerliches Gesetzbuch (ABGB)
JGS Nr. 946/1811 as amended BGBl. I Nr. 16/2020

...

Drittes Hauptstück—*Rechte zwischen Eltern und Kindern*

Erster Abschnitt—*Allgemeine Bestimmungen*

---

10 §5 of the Act on the Religious Upbringing of Children (*Gesetz über religiöse Kindererziehung*). See chapter 12.2.

11 See chapter 19.

§ 137—*Allgemeine Grundsätze*

(1) Eltern und Kinder haben einander beizustehen und mit Achtung zu begegnen. Die Rechte und Pflichten des Vaters und der Mutter sind, soweit nicht anderes bestimmt ist, gleich.
(2) Eltern haben das Wohl ihrer minderjährigen Kinder zu fördern, ihnen Fürsorge, Geborgenheit und eine sorgfältige Erziehung zu gewähren. Die Anwendung jeglicher Gewalt und die Zufügung körperlichen oder seelischen Leides sind unzulässig. Soweit tunlich und möglich sollen die Eltern die Obsorge einvernehmlich wahrnehmen.

§ 138—*Kindeswohl*

In allen das minderjährige Kind betreffenden Angelegenheiten, insbesondere der Obsorge und der persönlichen Kontakte, ist das Wohl des Kindes (Kindeswohl) als leitender Gesichtspunkt zu berücksichtigen und bestmöglich zu gewährleisten.
...

Vierter Abschnitt—*Obsorge*

§ 158—*Inhalt der Obsorge*

(1) Wer mit der Obsorge für ein minderjähriges Kind betraut ist, hat es zu pflegen und zu erziehen, sein Vermögen zu verwalten und es in diesen sowie allen anderen Angelegenheiten zu vertreten; Pflege und Erziehung sowie die Vermögensverwaltung umfassen auch die gesetzliche Vertretung in diesen Bereichen.
...

§ 160—*Pflege, Erziehung und Bestimmung des Aufenthalts des Kindes*

(1) Die Pflege des minderjährigen Kindes umfasst besonders die Wahrnehmung des körperlichen Wohles und der Gesundheit sowie die unmittelbare Aufsicht, die Erziehung besonders die Entfaltung der körperlichen, geistigen, seelischen und sittlichen Kräfte, die Förderung der Anlagen, Fähigkeiten, Neigungen und Entwicklungsmöglichkeiten des Kindes sowie dessen Ausbildung in Schule und Beruf.
...

§ 167—*Gesetzliche Vertretung des Kindes*

(1) Sind beide Eltern mit der Obsorge betraut, so ist jeder Elternteil für sich allein berechtigt und verpflichtet, das Kind zu vertreten; seine Vertretungshandlung ist selbst dann rechtswirksam, wenn der andere Elternteil mit ihr nicht einverstanden ist.
(2) Vertretungshandlungen und Einwilligungen eines Elternteils, die die Änderung des Vornamens oder des Familiennamens, den Eintritt in eine Kirche oder Religionsgesellschaft und den Austritt aus einer solchen, die Übergabe in fremde Pflege, den Erwerb einer Staatsangehörigkeit oder den Verzicht auf eine solche, die vorzeitige Lösung eines Lehr-, Ausbildungs- oder Dienstvertrags und die Anerkennung der Vaterschaft zu einem unehelichen Kind betreffen, bedürfen zu ihrer Rechtswirksamkeit der Zustimmung des anderen obsorgebetrauten Elternteils. Dies gilt nicht für die Entgegennahme von Willenserklärungen und Zustellstücken.
…

§ 179—*Obsorge bei Auflösung der Ehe und der häuslichen Gemeinschaft*

(1) Wird die Ehe oder die häusliche Gemeinschaft der Eltern aufgelöst, so bleibt die Obsorge beider Eltern aufrecht. Sie können jedoch vor Gericht eine Vereinbarung schließen, wonach ein Elternteil allein mit der Obsorge betraut wird oder die Obsorge eines Elternteils auf bestimmte Angelegenheiten beschränkt wird.
…

§ 181—*Entziehung oder Einschränkung der Obsorge*

(1) Gefährden die Eltern durch ihr Verhalten das Wohl des minderjährigen Kindes, so hat das Gericht, von wem immer es angerufen wird, die zur Sicherung des Wohles des Kindes nötigen Verfügungen zu treffen. Besonders darf das Gericht die Obsorge für das Kind ganz oder teilweise, auch gesetzlich vorgesehene Einwilligungs- und Zustimmungsrechte, entziehen. Im Einzelfall kann das Gericht auch eine gesetzlich erforderliche Einwilligung oder Zustimmung ersetzen, wenn keine gerechtfertigten Gründe für die Weigerung vorliegen.
…
(3) Die gänzliche oder teilweise Entziehung der Pflege und Erziehung oder der Verwaltung des Vermögens des Kindes schließt die Entziehung

der gesetzlichen Vertretung in dem jeweiligen Bereich mit ein; die gesetzliche Vertretung in diesen Bereichen kann für sich allein entzogen werden, wenn die Eltern oder der betreffende Elternteil ihre übrigen Pflichten erfüllen.
(4) Fordert das Gesetz die Einwilligung oder Zustimmung der mit Pflege und Erziehung betrauten Personen (Erziehungsberechtigten), so ist die Erklärung der mit der gesetzlichen Vertretung in diesem Bereich betrauten Person notwendig, aber auch hinreichend, sofern nicht Abweichendes bestimmt ist.
...

Pflegeeltern

§ 184

Pflegeeltern sind Personen, die die Pflege und Erziehung des Kindes ganz oder teilweise besorgen und zu denen eine dem Verhältnis zwischen leiblichen Eltern und Kindern nahe kommende Beziehung besteht oder hergestellt werden soll. Sie haben das Recht, in den die Person des Kindes betreffenden Verfahren Anträge zu stellen.

§ 185

(1) Das Gericht hat einem Pflegeelternpaar (Pflegeelternteil) auf seinen Antrag die Obsorge für das Kind ganz oder teilweise zu übertragen, wenn das Pflegeverhältnis nicht nur für kurze Zeit beabsichtigt ist und die Übertragung dem Wohl des Kindes entspricht. Die Regelungen über die Obsorge gelten dann für dieses Pflegeelternpaar (diesen Pflegeelternteil).
...

Fünfter Abschnitt—*Sonstige Rechte und Pflichten*
...

§ 189—*Informations-, Äußerungs- und Vertretungsrecht*

(1) Ein nicht mit der Obsorge betrauter Elternteil
1. ist durch die mit der Obsorge betraute Person von wichtigen Angelegenheiten, insbesondere von beabsichtigten Maßnahmen nach § 167 Abs. 2 und 3, rechtzeitig zu verständigen und kann sich hiezu in angemessener Frist äußern,

2. hat den mit der Obsorge betrauten Elternteil in Angelegenheiten des täglichen Lebens zu vertreten sowie das Kind zu pflegen und zu erziehen, soweit das die Umstände erfordern und sich das Kind rechtmäßig bei ihm aufhält.
Eine Äußerung nach Z 1 ist in jedem Fall zu berücksichtigen, wenn der darin ausgedrückte Wunsch dem Wohl des Kindes entspricht.
(2) Wenn der nicht mit der Obsorge betraute Elternteil bei der Wahrnehmung seiner Rechte und Pflichten nach Abs. 1 das Wohl des Kindes gefährdet oder diese Rechte rechtsmissbräuchlich oder in einer für den anderen Elternteil oder das Kind nicht zumutbaren Weise in Anspruch nimmt, hat das Gericht diese Rechte auf Antrag, sofern das Wohl des Kindes gefährdet wird, auch von Amts wegen, einzuschränken oder zu entziehen. Die Rechte nach Abs. 1 entfallen, wenn der mit der Obsorge nicht betraute Elternteil grundlos das Recht des Kindes auf persönliche Kontakte ablehnt.
…

Case Law

Case 1: A unilateral legal allocation of parental custody to one parent, especially to the father, without a specific reason arising out of the person of the other parent and without regard to the child's welfare is contrary to the Austrian *ordre public*: OGH 7. 11. 1974, 7Ob218/74; 4. 12. 1974, 5Ob296/74; 15.06.1976, 3Ob224/75.

Case 2: It cannot generally be 'regarded as unlawful or contrary to the child's wellbeing' if a father raises a child in his religion. In the present case, the Islamic education of a daughter, born in 1981, went back to an original agreement with the Christian mother. According to the overriding principle of the child's welfare, it must be ensured that the father has the basic ability to bring it up and that the child concerned has already internalised the educational principles of the father to such an extent that changes in the principles of education would be associated with severe psychological stress.

The younger child, born in 1985, had previously grown up with the mother, who was granted sole parental rights. In this case the other parent had a mere right to information. The aim of this provision is to avoid, in the best interests of the child, disputes between the parents about certain measures that must be taken for the purpose of raising the child. Measures taken by the parent with the sole right of legal representation, such as baptism and the determination of the religious education, therefore, require neither the approval nor the consent of the other parent: OGH 22. 9. 1988, 7Ob655/88, 7Ob656/88.

Case 3: The judicial or administrative authorities of the state of habitual residence of an infant primarily have the power to take measures directed at the protection of his person or property (Article 1 of the Hague Protection of Minors Convention[12]). The authorities of the state of the infant's nationality have to be informed and, in accordance with Article 4 section 4, the measures taken by that state shall override any measures which may have been taken by the authorities of the state where the infant has his habitual residence. According to Article 16 of the Convention, the application of these provisions can be declined by the Contracting States only if such application is manifestly contrary to the *ordre public* of the state of habitual residence. In the present case, the Turkish minor had been living with a foster family in Austria for more than four years and, apart from his nationality, had no ties with Turkey because of the lack of reference people living there. By reason of the intended transfer of custody to a Turkish authority in Turkey, there was a real danger that he would be traumatised. There was, thus, a blatant threat to the best interests of the child, which is the supreme maxim of guardianship proceedings, so that the application of the reservation clause in Article 16 was obvious: OGH 28. 8. 2013, 6Ob138/13g.

Case 4: The two youngest of five children in a Turkish family had been placed in their foster families, first in crisis care and then in permanent care, by reason of the parents' lack of parenting skills in the completely neglected household. They had established relationships with their foster parents such that they would not be able to cope if they were broken off, which would endanger them. Their return to their parents would pose a risk *per se* because of their youth and the neglect they had suffered (at the time of acceptance). Since the children had had to be taken away from their parents because they had been neglected by them, the accusations of 'forced Christianisation' and 'alienation from Turkishness' were inappropriate. The parents' fears in this regard were also not covered by the facts. The claimed advantage of growing up in the extended family and cultural environment to which the children belonged by reason of their origin, with people who were strangers to them, could not justify the risk of losing their current and familiar living and relationship environment: OGH 22. 10. 2014, 3Ob179/14s.

18.3 Private International Law

Austrian international private law is codified in the Federal Law of 15 June 1978 on private international law (IPRG). Personal status is basically determ-

12 Convention concerning the Powers of Authority and the Law applicable in respect of the Protection of Infants of 5 October 1961 (*Übereinkommen über die Zuständigkeit der*

ined by nationality; for Austrian citizens it is under Austrian law (§ 9 of the IPRG).

18.3.1 *The* Ordre public *Proviso*

As far as marriages of/with nationals of an Islamic country practising Islamic law are concerned, that law should be applied unless the *ordre public* proviso comes into play. In accordance with § 6 of the IPRG, the *ordre public* proviso means that 'a provision of foreign law shall not be applied if this application would lead to a result that is incompatible with the fundamental values of the Austrian legal system.'

The courts have developed a set of principles for the application of the *ordre public* proviso. The issues are often related to the application of 'Islamic law' or are usually brought into connection with it. In addition to constitutionally protected basic values, the *ordre public* proviso covers monogamy, the prohibition of child marriage and marital coercion as well as the protection of child welfare under the child custody laws. Since it is an exception contrary to the principle of the equivalence of all legal systems, the courts have to make the most sparing use of the proviso. A mere deviation from Austrian provisions is not sufficient to justify the application of the *ordre public* proviso.

18.3.2 *Matrimonial Law*

In accordance with § 16 section 1 of the IPRG, a marriage in Austria is formally valid only if entered into before the state registrar, even if the law governing a foreign fiancé(e) permits another form of marriage. Religious marriages (such as 'Imam marriages') have no legal consequences. Foreign religious marriages can be recognised only when they have legal effect in accordance with the relevant state law. Turkish Imam marriages in Austria, although they have a certain importance for migrants of Turkish citizenship, therefore, are legally invalid.

In accordance with § 17 section 1 of the IPRG, the preconditions for marriage, the nullity and the annulment of the marriage for each member of the engaged couple are to be judged according to his/her personal status. The personal status of a fiancé at the time of marriage is the relevant one. When foreign law is being applied, the *ordre public* generally allows only a minimal reduction

---

Behörden und das anzuwendende Recht auf dem Gebiet des Schutzes von Minderjährigen), BGBl. Nr. 46/1975.

of the legal marriageable age of 16 years.[13] The marriage of a young woman under 14 years is in any case against *ordre public*.[14]

It is contrary to Austrian *ordre public* if a marriage is based directly or indirectly on serious pressure exerted on one of the parties.[15]

Marriages by proxy are permissible in Islamic law. As long as the person is stated in the declaration to be a proxy, it is a question of form and it is sufficient to satisfy the relevant provisions of local law. A representation of a party (with the authority of partner selection or a discretion of the representative to conclude or not) is contrary to public order.[16] Therefore, the judicial confirmation and registration of a traditional Islamic marriage as a civil marriage made by proxies does not constitute a marriage by proxy, but merely the confirmation of the legal validity of an existing marriage.

The secularised marriage law does not include impediments based on religion. Therefore, the foreign legal impediment of a marriage, a divorce for religious reasons and annulment on the grounds of religion—especially in the case of an interreligious marriage of Muslim women—are not in accordance with Austrian *ordre public*.

The conditions and the personal and legal effects of a divorce are to be judged in accordance with the matrimonial law applicable at the time of divorce (§ 20 section 1 of the IPRG). As in other European countries, problems often arise in the application of Islamic law in the field of Islamic divorce law. The focus of divorce-related problems of Islamic law is on the *ṭalāq* divorce. The recognition of a unilateral repudiation of a wife by her husband in principal goes against Austrian *ordre public*. A content-related review of family law matters in accordance with the conflict-of-law provisions of private international law must be distinguished from the formal recognition of foreign judgments. The procedures for recognising them on the one hand are based on the mutual recognition of judicial decisions according to EU law[17] and on the other on autonomous Austrian provisions under which a foreign judgment on divorce

13 Cf. § 1 EheG, see 18.1.

14 For the actual discussion regarding a possible reform see Melcher, Martina, '(Un-)Wirksamkeit von Kinderehen in Österreich,' EF-Z 50 (2018), 103–108.

15 Since the amendment of the Criminal Code of 2006, forced marriages have beene classified as severe coercion under § 106 section 1 nr. 3. Another measure against forced marriages of girls—implementing Directive 2003/86/EC on the right to family reunification—was the increasing of the age limit of spouses to 21 years for claims for family reunification with effect from 1 January 2010 (prohibition of 'import of underage brides').

16 See Verschraegen, Bea, *Kommentar zum ABGB, Ergänzungsband § 16 IPRG* (3rd ed. Vienna: Manz, 2004), Rz. 4.

17 Council Regulation (EU) No. 1259/2010 of 20 December 2010 implementing enhanced

and other forms of dissolution of marriage is recognised if it is final and there is no reason for refusing recognition.[18] A divorce resulting from a unilateral declaration made by one of the spouses before a religious court is not valid, as a private divorce does not come within the substantive scope of Council Regulation (EU) No. 1259/2010. It has to be judged according to national law.[19] Due to the broad understanding in Austrian jurisprudence of the term 'judgment', which is not limited to constitutive decisions of a foreign state authority, decisions in which an authority has only participated in their registration process are to be assessed according to the rules of recognition[20] and not just according to international private law.

18.3.3 *Parent and Child Law*

The effects of the legitimacy and the legitimation of a child are to be judged according to its personal status at the time of birth.[21] Legitimation requires the determination of parentage. In the case of the recognition of legitimacy according to Islamic law, both the parentage and the legitimacy are recognised.

The preconditions for adoption and its termination are to be judged according the personal status of each adopter and the personal status of the child (§ 26 section 1 of the IPRG). The effects of the adoption are assessed according to the personal status of the adopter, for an adoption by spouses according to the law which is relevant for legal consequences of the marriage (§ 26 section 2 of the IPRG). The Islamic adoption ban is taken into account insofar as the adoption of an adult person is not permitted if that person's personal status either generally (e.g. if the legal institute of the adoption is not known) or because of the adoptee's age does not permit it. Such people cannot be effectively adopted in Austria.[22]

---

cooperation in the area of the law applicable to divorce and legal separation ('Rome III Regulation').

18 § 97 of the Act on non-adversarial Procedure (*Bundesgesetz über das gerichtliche Verfahren in Rechtsangelegenheiten außer Streitsachen, Außerstreitgesetz*), BGBl. I Nr. 111/2003 as amended BGBl. I Nr. 38/2019. In addition, there are also cross-national agreements, such as the Hague Convention on Adoption, which cannot be discussed here.

19 Cf. ECJ 20. 2. 2018, Case C-372/16, Soha Sahyoumi/Raja Mamisch.

20 See § 97 of the Act on Non-adversarial Procedure (*Bundesgesetz über das gerichtliche Verfahren in Rechtsangelegenheiten außer Streitsachen, Außerstreitgesetz*), BGBl. I Nr. 111/2003 as amended BGBl. I Nr. 38/2019, case 1.

21 This provision is important, for example, for the questions of care and upbringing of a child, its legal representation by one or both parents, the regulation of parental authority after divorce and mutual maintenance claims.

22 Cf. the explanatory notes (NR GP XXII, RV 471: https://www.parlament.gv.at/PAKT/VHG/XXII/I/I_00471/fname_020121.pdf, pp. 11, 34 [last accessed April 17th, 2020]) to the Family

Bundesgesetz vom 15. Juni 1978 über das internationale Privatrecht (IPR-Gesetz)
BGBl. Nr. 304/1978 as amended BGBl. I Nr. 72/2019

…

§ 6—*Vorbehaltsklausel* (*ordre public*)

Eine Bestimmung des fremden Rechtes ist nicht anzuwenden, wenn ihre Anwendung zu einem Ergebnis führen würde, das mit den Grundwertungen der österreichischen Rechtsordnung unvereinbar ist. An ihrer Stelle ist erforderlichenfalls die entsprechende Bestimmung des österreichischen Rechtes anzuwenden.

Case Law[23]

Case 1: An essential prerequisite for the application of the reservation clause is that the result and not merely the foreign law itself is offensive: OGH 24. 9. 1998, 6Ob242/98a.

Case 2: The content of the protected fundamental values of Austrian law cannot be defined in detail and is also subject to change over time. Outside the constitutionally protected basic values, for example, marriage, the prohibition of child marriage, and forced marriage, the protection of the wellbeing of children under child law and the prohibition of the exploitation of the economically and socially weaker party belong to the scope of protection of *ordre public*: OGH 10. 7. 1986, 7Ob600/86.

Case 3: If for a woman living in Austria there is no chance of her marriage situation being resolved, despite the breakdown of the marriage and the intolerability of further cohabitation, then the result of applying foreign law—in this case *ja'fari* (shiite) law to which Lebanese law refers for dissolution—contravenes Austrian *ordre public*: OGH 24. 9. 1998, 6Ob242/98a.

Case 4: The nullity of a marriage provided in foreign law for reasons of religion contravenes Austrian *ordre public* because the recognition of such a ground for nullity of a marriage would lead to legal consequences which did not accord with the secular concept of Austrian law: VwGH 14. 5. 1984, 84/12/0024; VwGH 30. 1. 1991, 89/01/0276.

---

and Succession Law Amendment Act 2004 (*Familien- und Erbrechtsänderungsgesetz*—FamErbRÄG 2004, BGBl. I Nr. 58/2004).

23 For the application of the *ordre-public* proviso in divorce cases cf. below.

Case 5: The mere fact of the recognition of a traditional marriage with subsequent state registration with legal effect from the date of the traditional marriage in foreign law does not violate the basic judgments of the Austrian legal system: VwGH 6. 9. 2018; Ra 2018/18/0094.

Case 6: A unilateral legal allocation of parental custody to a parent, especially to the father, without a specific reason emanating from the person of the other parent and without regard to the child's welfare is contrary to Austrian *ordre public*: OGH 7. 11. 1974, 7Ob218/74; 4. 12. 1974, 5Ob296/74; 15. 6. 1976, 3Ob224/75.

§ 9—*Personalstatut einer natürlichen Person*

(1) Das Personalstatut einer natürlichen Person ist das Recht des Staates, dem die Person angehört. Hat eine Person neben einer fremden Staatsangehörigkeit auch die österreichische Staatsbürgerschaft, so ist diese maßgebend. Für andere Mehrstaater ist die Staatsangehörigkeit des Staates maßgebend, zu dem die stärkste Beziehung besteht.
(2) Ist eine Person staatenlos oder kann ihre Staatsangehörigkeit nicht geklärt werden, so ist ihr Personalstatut das Recht des Staates, in dem sie den gewöhnlichen Aufenthalt hat.
(3) Das Personalstatut einer Person, die Flüchtling im Sinn der für Österreich geltenden internationalen Übereinkommen ist oder deren Beziehungen zu ihrem Heimatstaat aus vergleichbar schwerwiegenden Gründen abgebrochen sind, ist das Recht des Staates, in dem sie ihren Wohnsitz, mangels eines solchen ihren gewöhnlichen Aufenthalt hat; eine Verweisung dieses Rechtes auf das Recht des Heimatstaates (§ 5) ist unbeachtlich.

…

Dritter Abschnitt—*Familienrecht*

A. *Eherecht*

§ 16—*Form der Eheschließung*

(1) Die Form einer Eheschließung im Inland ist nach den inländischen Formvorschriften zu beurteilen.
(2) Die Form einer Eheschließung im Ausland ist nach dem Personalstatut jedes der Verlobten zu beurteilen; es genügt jedoch die Einhaltung der Formvorschriften des Ortes der Eheschließung.

§ 17—*Voraussetzungen der Eheschließung*

(1) Die Voraussetzungen der Eheschließung sowie die der Ehenichtigkeit und der Aufhebung sind für jeden der Verlobten nach seinem Personalstatut zu beurteilen.[24]
(2) Ist durch eine für den österreichischen Rechtsbereich wirksame Entscheidung eine Ehe für nichtig erklärt, aufgehoben, geschieden oder als nicht bestehend festgestellt worden, so darf nicht allein deshalb eine neue Eheschließung untersagt oder eine neue Ehe für nichtig erklärt werden, weil die Entscheidung nach dem Personalstatut eines oder beider Verlobten bzw. Ehegatten nicht anerkannt wird. Dies gilt sinngemäß im Fall der Todeserklärung oder der Beweisführung des Todes.

§ 18—*Persönliche Rechtswirkungen der Ehe*

(1) Die persönlichen Rechtswirkungen einer Ehe sind zu beurteilen
1. nach dem gemeinsamen, mangels eines solchen nach dem letzten gemeinsamen Personalstatut der Ehegatten, sofern es einer von ihnen beibehalten hat,
2. sonst nach dem Recht des Staates, in dem beide Ehegatten ihren gewöhnlichen Aufenthalt haben, mangels eines solchen nach dem Recht des Staates, in dem beide ihren letzten gewöhnlichen Aufenthalt gehabt haben, sofern ihn einer von ihnen beibehalten hat.
(2) Ist eine Ehe nicht für den Bereich des im Abs. 1 bezeichneten Rechtes, wohl aber für den österreichischen Rechtsbereich zustande gekommen, so sind die persönlichen Rechtswirkungen nach österreichischem Recht zu beurteilen. Haben jedoch die Eheleute eine stärkere Beziehung zu einem dritten Staat, nach dessen Recht die Ehe ebenfalls Wirkungen entfaltet, so ist statt des österreichischen Rechtes das Recht dieses Staates maßgebend.

§ 19—*Ehegüterrecht*

Das Ehegüterrecht ist nach dem Recht zu beurteilen, das die Parteien ausdrücklich bestimmen, mangels einer solchen Rechtswahl nach dem zur Zeit der Eheschließung für die persönlichen Rechtswirkungen der Ehe maßgebenden Recht.

---

24 The personal status of the fiancé at the time of the marriage is decisive. A later change of status is irrelevant (§ 7).

§ 20—*Ehescheidung*

(1) Die Voraussetzungen und die Wirkungen der Scheidung einer Ehe sind nach dem für die persönlichen Rechtswirkungen der Ehe maßgebenden Recht im Zeitpunkt der Ehescheidung zu beurteilen.
(2) Kann nach diesem Recht die Ehe auf Grund der geltend gemachten Tatsachen nicht geschieden werden oder liegt keiner der Anknüpfungspunkte des § 18 vor, so ist die Scheidung nach dem Personalstatut des klagenden Ehegatten im Zeitpunkt der Ehescheidung zu beurteilen.

Case Law

Case 1: If for a woman living in Austria there is no chance of her marriage situation being resolved, despite the breakdown of the marriage and the intolerability of further cohabitation, then the result of applying foreign law—in this case *ja'fari* (shiite) law to which Lebanese law refers for dissolution—contravenes Austrian *ordre public*: OGH 24. 9. 1998, 6Ob242/98a;

Case 2: The judicial confirmation and registration of a traditional Islamic marriage as a civil marriage with retrospective effect, which was initiated on behalf of the spouses by their deputies under Syrian law, does not constitute a marriage by proxy, but merely the confirmation of the legal validity of the marriage: BVwG 28. 4. 2016, W144 2125312-1; VwGH 6. 9. 2018, Ra 2018/18/0094; BVwG W240 2158018-2.

Case 3: If, in accordance with § 18 section 1 nr. 1 of the IPRG, Austrian substantive law has to be applied—for instance because the two parties are Austrian citizens—a separation has to be carried out by court decision. In the case concerned the man had claimed to have legally divorced his wife during a stay in Pakistan by unilateral repudiation (*ṭalāq*) and, with the application for recognition he had submitted a certificate of the Pakistani authorities who confirmed that the private divorce had been issued validly. Since Austrian substantive law prohibits marital separation by contract, foreign private separations have no effect: OGH 31. 8. 2006, 6Ob189/06x.

Case 4: If a family court allows only the husband to contact an office for the registration of divorce, it is a *ṭalāq* and cannot be recognised. Even if a woman has the right to appeal to the court to be allowed to divorce her husband, the only way to a divorce is a declaration by the husband. If he refuses, the court can dissolve the marriage only by acting as the husband's legal representative. In such cases divorce is always a declaration of the man, even if the man has given his wife the right to represent him in it. Although the court is involved, this private Iranian form of divorce, therefore, cannot not be recognised: OGH 13. 10. 2011, OGH 6Ob69/11g.

Case 5: Post-divorce maintenance is determined by the statute of divorce. Even if the applicable foreign law refuses the payment of maintenance after divorce, that is not necessarily a violation of the domestic *ordre public*. In this case, Saudi Arabian marriage law had to be applied, which refers the consequences of divorce to the *sharia*. If there is a legal divorce, the woman is entitled to maintenance for only the so-called 'waiting period' of three months after the divorce.

It does not matter whether or not the applicable law awards a former spouse maintenance in principle; the essential question is whether in the given situation the fact that the spouse does not receive maintenance (for instance where both sides are equally responsible for the breakdown of the marriage) violates Austrian fundamental values. Thus, a foreign law which limits maintenance to three months after the divorce does not in its result unacceptably contravene—which would be necessary for the application of the *ordre public* proviso—fundamental values of the Austrian legal system: OGH 28. 2. 2011, 9Ob34/10f.

B. *Kindschaftsrecht*

§ 21—*Eheliche Abstammung*

Die Voraussetzungen der Ehelichkeit eines Kindes und deren Bestreitung sind nach dem Personalstatut zu beurteilen, das die Ehegatten im Zeitpunkt der Geburt des Kindes oder, wenn die Ehe vorher aufgelöst worden ist, im Zeitpunkt der Auflösung gehabt haben. Bei verschiedenem Personalstatut der Ehegatten ist das Personalstatut des Kindes zum Zeitpunkt der Geburt maßgebend.

§ 24—*Wirkungen der Ehelichkeit und der Legitimation*

Die Wirkungen der Ehelichkeit und der Legitimation eines Kindes sind nach dessen Personalstatut zu beurteilen.

…

§ 26—*Annahme an Kindesstatt*

(1) Die Voraussetzungen der Annahme an Kindesstatt und der Beendigung der Wahlkindschaft sind nach dem Personalstatut jedes Annehmenden und dem Personalstatut des Kindes zu beurteilen. Ist das Kind nicht

eigenberechtigt, so ist sein Personalstatut nur hinsichtlich der Zustimmung des Kindes oder eines Dritten, zu dem das Kind in einem familienrechtlichen Verhältnis steht, maßgebend.
(2) Die Wirkungen der Annahme an Kindesstatt sind nach dem Personalstatut des Annehmenden, bei Annahme durch Ehegatten nach dem für die persönlichen Rechtswirkungen der Ehe maßgebenden Recht, nach dem Tod eines der Ehegatten nach dem Personalstatut des anderen Ehegatten zu beurteilen.

Case Law

Case 1: According to the Syrian law applicable in the present case, the relevant family law is the religious law of the person concerned. Islamic law, which applies to the second applicant, an adult Muslim, knows no possibility of adoption at all. Since the impossibility of adopting a foreign adult does not violate Austrian *ordre public per se*, there is no need to check whether the Syrian regulation is discriminatory in differentiating according to religion or contrary to the principle of secularity: OGH 22.10.2010, 9Ob70/10z.

Bundesgesetz über das gerichtliche Verfahren in Rechtsangelegenheiten außer Streitsachen (Außerstreitgesetz—AußStrG),

BGBl. I Nr. 111/2003 as amended BGBl. I Nr. 38/2019

Fünfter Abschnitt—*Anerkennung ausländischer Entscheidungen über den Bestand einer Ehe*

§ 97—*Anerkennung Verweigerungsgründe*

(1) Eine ausländische Entscheidung über die Trennung ohne Auflösung des Ehebandes, die Ehescheidung oder die Ungültigerklärung einer Ehe sowie über die Feststellung des Bestehens oder Nichtbestehens einer Ehe wird in Österreich anerkannt, wenn sie rechtskräftig ist und kein Grund zur Verweigerung der Anerkennung vorliegt. Die Anerkennung kann als Vorfrage selbständig beurteilt werden, ohne dass es eines besonderen Verfahrens bedarf.
(2) Die Anerkennung der Entscheidung ist zu verweigern, wenn
1. sie den Grundwertungen der österreichischen Rechtsordnung (ordre public) offensichtlich widerspricht;
2. das rechtliche Gehör eines der Ehegatten nicht gewahrt wurde, es sei denn, er ist mit der Entscheidung offenkundig einverstanden;

3. die Entscheidung mit einer österreichischen oder einer früheren die Voraussetzungen für eine Anerkennung in Österreich erfüllenden Entscheidung unvereinbar ist, mit der die betreffende Ehe getrennt, geschieden, für ungültig erklärt oder das Bestehen oder Nichtbestehen der Ehe festgestellt worden ist;
4. die erkennende Behörde bei Anwendung österreichischen Rechts international nicht zuständig gewesen wäre.

Case Law

Case 1: Because of very different procedural laws, the term 'judgment' is to be interpreted broadly and not to be limited to constitutive decisions of a foreign state authority. It is sufficient that the court has been involved in the divorce even if only by holding reconciliation proceedings or by registration of the divorce: VwGH 14.5.1984, 84/12/0024; OGH 31. 8. 2006, 6Ob189/06x; 29. 1. 2010, 1Ob138/09i.

Case 2: Where a woman's subsequent consent is declared unilaterally by the husband, the law does not provide for any possibility of validation by the parties (§ 97 Abs 2 Z 1 AußStrG): OGH 28. 6. 2007, 3Ob130/07z.

Case 3: If a family court allows only the husband to contact an office for the registration of divorce, it is a *ṭalāq* and cannot be recognised. Even if a woman has the right to appeal to the court to be allowed to divorce her husband, the only way to a divorce is a declaration by the husband. If he refuses, the court can dissolve the marriage only by acting as the husband's legal representative. In such cases divorce is always a declaration of the man, even if the man has given his wife the right to represent him in it. Although the court is involved, this private Iranian form of divorce, therefore, cannot not be recognised: OGH 13. 10. 2011, 6Ob69/11g.

CHAPTER 19

Criminal Law

19.1 Introduction

Religion plays a role in a number of offences, where either religious peace is the immediate object of protection or religion is the cause of an increased threat of punishment. Recently, some criminal offences which are associated with Islamic traditions, like female genital mutilation and forced marriage, have been added in public discussions, even if they can also be found in non-Islamic cultural milieus.

Criminal law is one of the few areas where the different legal categories of churches and religious communities have no significance.[1]

The Criminal Code does not specifically provide for offences which are aggravated by religious motivation or as a matter of conscience. Neither Austrian doctrine nor the courts deal thoroughly with the problems arising from offences committed because of the religious convictions of offenders; this issue is addressed mainly from the perspective of guilty knowledge. According to prevailing opinion, the fundamental assumption is that offenders are conscious of the wrongful nature of their acts. Thus, error as to the prohibited nature of an action is regularly precluded.

19.2 The Protection of Religious Peace

There is no offence corresponding to blasphemy as such. Blasphemy was abolished in the great revision of the Penal Code in 1975 (StGB), though this had already long been a field of 'dead law.' Since then the Penal Code has simply provided for 'disparaging religious doctrines' (§ 188 of the StGB).

This provision aims to protect both practices of religious cults and manifestations of personal convictions from interference and compulsion; in other words, it aims, primarily, at the peaceful co-existence of citizens with different religious and philosophical convictions.

However, this also implies the protection of the religious feelings of believers. As far as the typology is concerned, this offence represents an 'abstract strict-liability tort' and actual realisation is not required.

1 See chapter 2.3.1.

A more serious punishment is provided for a person who, publicly and in a manner calculated to endanger public order or that is perceptible by a broad public, provokes or explicitly incites violence towards a church or religious community or towards another group defined by the criteria of, inter alia, religion or belief, or towards a member of such a group (§ 283 section 1 of the StGB).

In accordance with § 189 of the StGB the desecration of a place of worship or a sacred object of any religion and the hindrance or disruption of a sacred service are to be punished.

19.3 Religion as Qualifying Element of an Offence

Punishment is aggravated for two offences if they are, inter alia, committed in combination with religion. These are the causing of severe damage to property dedicated to the sacred service or religious worship of a church or religious community, or to a grave or other burial place, a tomb or a memorial located in a cemetery or in a place used for religious practice (§ 126 of the StGB). Severe theft committed at a place used for religious worship or of an object dedicated to the sacred services or religious worship of a church or religious community (§ 128 of the StGB) also carries an aggravated punishment.

19.4 Confessional Secret[2]

Criminal law takes account of the confessional secret with regard to the 'omission to prevent an action liable to prosecution' (§ 286 section 1). § 286 section 2 provides for the impunity of the delinquent 'in so far as he learned about the imminent action on the basis of information confided to him in his capacity as spiritual minister'. This means that it is up to the spiritual minister to decide whether or not he makes use of this exemption.

19.5 Female Genital Mutilation

In accordance with § 85 section 1 no. 2a of the StGB genital mutilation or any other genital injury which causes a lasting impairment of sexual sensation

2 For the procedural rules providing for the protection of the confessional secret see chapter 14.2.

qualifies as a serious physical injury with serious continuing effects and is, therefore, subject to a heightened threat of punishment. Such physical injury cannot be justified even with the injured person's consent, as it is illegal to agree to it (§ 90 section 3).[3]

19.6 Forced Marriage

The 2006 Criminal Law Amendment Act[4] made it possible to act consistently against all persons involved in a forced marriage, especially family members (§ 106 section 1 no. 3). This is intended to emphasise that marriage under coercion, like prostitution and participation in a pornographic performance, violates particularly important interests of the coerced person and, therefore, constitutes severe duress. The legislator sees the equivalence of the coercion goals in the profound interference with the self-determination and sexual integrity of the victim connected with forced marriage.

19.7 Cruelty to Animals

Cruelty to animals in accordance with § 222 of the StGB presupposes cruelly mistreating an animal and inflicting unnecessary torture on it. These conditions are not met in the case of ritual slaughter.[5]

Bundesgesetz vom 23. Jänner 1974 über die mit gerichtlicher Strafe bedrohten Handlungen (Strafgesetzbuch—StGB)

BGBl. Nr. 60/1974 idF BGBl. I Nr. 111/2019

Körperverletzung mit schweren Dauerfolgen
§ 85.
(1) Wer einen anderen am Körper misshandelt und dadurch fahrlässig für immer oder für lange Zeit

3 B. Schinkele, "Religionsfreiheit, Reichweite und Grenzen im Kontext religiös-kultureller Praktiken—unter besonderer Berücksichtigung von Female Genital Mutilation und Zirkumzision," in *Interkulturell kompetent. Ein Handbuch für Ärztinnen und Ärzte*, ed. M. Peintinger (Vienna: facultas.wuv, 2011), 103–118.

4 *Strafrechtsänderungsgesetz* 2006, BGBl. I Nr. 56/2006.

5 Cf. chapter 16.1.

…
2a. eine Verstümmelung oder sonstige Verletzung der Genitalien, die geeignet ist, eine nachhaltige Beeinträchtigung des sexuellen Empfindens herbeizuführen, oder
…
ist mit Freiheitsstrafe von sechs Monaten bis zu fünf Jahren zu bestrafen.

Einwilligung des Verletzten
§ 90.
(1) Eine Körperverletzung oder Gefährdung der körperlichen Sicherheit ist nicht rechtswidrig, wenn der Verletzte oder Gefährdete in sie einwilligt und die Verletzung oder Gefährdung als solche nicht gegen die guten Sitten verstößt.
(2) Die von einem Arzt an einer Person mit deren Einwilligung vorgenommene Sterilisation ist nicht rechtswidrig, wenn entweder die Person bereits das fünfundzwanzigste Lebensjahr vollendet hat oder der Eingriff aus anderen Gründen nicht gegen die guten Sitten verstößt.
(3) In eine Genitalverstümmelung (§ 85 Abs. 1 Z 2a) kann nicht eingewilligt werden.

Schwere Nötigung
§ 106.
(1) Wer eine Nötigung begeht, indem er
…
3. die genötigte Person zur Eheschließung, zur Begründung einer eingetragenen Partnerschaft, zur Prostitution oder zur Mitwirkung an einer pornographischen Darbietung (§ 215a Abs. 3) oder sonst zu einer Handlung, Duldung oder Unterlassung veranlasst, die besonders wichtige Interessen der genötigten oder einer dritten Person verletzt,
ist mit Freiheitsstrafe von sechs Monaten bis zu fünf Jahren zu bestrafen.
(2) Hat die Tat den Selbstmord oder einen Selbstmordversuch der genötigten oder einer anderen Person, gegen die sich die Gewalt oder gefährliche Drohung richtet, zur Folge, so ist der Täter mit Freiheitsstrafe von einem bis zu zehn Jahren zu bestrafen.
…

Schwere Sachbeschädigung
§ 126.
(1) Mit Freiheitsstrafe bis zu zwei Jahren ist zu bestrafen, wer eine Sachbeschädigung begeht

1. an einer Sache, die dem Gottesdienst oder der Verehrung durch eine im Inland bestehende Kirche oder Religionsgesellschaft gewidmet ist,
2. an einem Grab, einer anderen Beisetzungsstätte, einem Grabmal oder an einer Totengedenkstätte, die sich in einem Friedhof oder einem der Religionsübung dienenden Raum befindet,
...

Case Law

Case 1: Churches, chapels, synagogues and mosques are by their very nature dedicated to worship. Damage to the outer walls of such buildings, therefore, qualifies as serious damage to property under §126 section 1 no. 1 of the StGB. It is not necessary for the building to be exclusively dedicated to worship or veneration and or for an object to be indispensable for the rite: OGH 3. 2. 1983, 13Os 189/82.

Schwerer Diebstahl
§128.
(1) Mit Freiheitsstrafe bis zu drei Jahren ist zu bestrafen, wer einen Diebstahl begeht
3. während einer Feuersbrunst, einer Überschwemmung oder einer allgemeinen oder doch dem Bestohlenen zugestoßenen Bedrängnis oder unter Ausnützung eines Zustands des Bestohlenen, der ihn hilflos macht,
4. in einem der Religionsübung dienenden Raum oder an einer Sache, die dem Gottesdienst oder der Verehrung durch eine im Inland bestehende Kirche oder Religionsgesellschaft gewidmet ist,

Achter Abschnitt
Strafbare Handlungen gegen den religiösen Frieden und die Ruhe der Toten

Herabwürdigung religiöser Lehren
§188.
Wer öffentlich eine Person oder eine Sache, die den Gegenstand der Verehrung einer im Inland bestehenden Kirche oder Religionsgesellschaft bildet, oder eine Glaubenslehre, einen gesetzlich zulässigen Brauch oder eine gesetzlich zulässige Einrichtung einer solchen Kirche oder Religionsgesellschaft unter Umständen herabwürdigt oder verspottet, unter denen sein Verhalten geeignet ist, berechtigtes Ärgernis zu erregen, ist mit Freiheitsstrafe bis zu sechs Monaten oder mit Geldstrafe bis zu 360 Tagessätzen zu bestrafen.

Case Law

Case 1: An offence must be committed in public and under circumstances where the behaviour is likely to give rise to justified annoyance. The term 'annoyance' is to be understood as a profound feeling, which is caused by the violation of religious values and directed against the offending act or its author: OLG Graz, 12. 12. 1983, 8 BS 377/83.

Case 2: In matters of religious belief, the state has an obligation to prevent the making of critical statements that believers find extremely insulting and provocative. In a public lecture, the Prophet Muhammad, a person of veneration in Islam, was accused of a pathological sexual preference (paedophilia) without an objective examination and debate having taken place. This is not only a disturbing, shocking or provocative statement or view in the context of a factual dispute, but an unjustified and insulting attack on Islam, and is, therefore, an offence in accordance with § 188 StGB: OGH 11. 12. 2013, 15 Os 52/12d.[6]

Störung einer Religionsübung

§ 189.

(1) Wer mit Gewalt oder durch Drohung mit Gewalt den gesetzlich zulässigen Gottesdienst oder einzelne solche gottesdienstliche Handlungen einer im Inland bestehenden Kirche oder Religionsgesellschaft hindert oder stört, ist mit Freiheitsstrafe bis zu zwei Jahren zu bestrafen.

(2) Wer

1. an einem Ort, der der gesetzlich zulässigen Religionsübung einer im Inland bestehenden Kirche oder Religionsgesellschaft gewidmet ist,
2. bei dem gesetzlich zulässigen öffentlichen Gottesdienst oder einzelnen gesetzlich zulässigen öffentlichen gottesdienstlichen Handlungen einer im Inland bestehenden Kirche oder Religionsgesellschaft oder
3. mit einem dem gesetzlich zulässigen Gottesdienst einer im Inland bestehenden Kirche oder Religionsgesellschaft unmittelbar gewidmeten Gegenstand

auf eine Weise Unfug treibt, die geeignet ist, berechtigtes Ärgernis zu erregen, ist mit Freiheitsstrafe bis zu sechs Monaten oder mit Geldstrafe bis zu 360 Tagessätzen zu bestrafen.

6 Cf. ECHR 25. 10. 2018, appl 38,450/12.

Elfter Abschnitt
Tierquälerei

Tierquälerei
§ 222.
(1) Wer ein Tier

1. roh misshandelt oder ihm unnötige Qualen zufügt,
...
ist mit Freiheitsstrafe bis zu zwei Jahre zu bestrafen.
...

Case Law

Case 1: Slaughtering anaesthetised animals in accordance with Jewish and Islamic religious provisions is not cruelty to animals within the meaning of § 222 section 1 of the Criminal Code. The ritual slaughter of sheep exhibits socially adequate behaviour that rules out illegality. Therefore, as a negative element of the offence of cruelty to animals, the slaughter of animals according to the religious precepts of Muslims and Jews cannot constitute the above-mentioned crime (cf. VwSlg 10.666/1897; VwSlg 5248A/1907): VfGH 17. 12. 1998, VfSlg 15394/1998; in this sense also OGH 28. 3. 1996, 15 Os 27/96.

Zwanzigster Abschnitt
Strafbare Handlungen gegen den öffentlichen Frieden

Verhetzung
§ 283.
(1) Wer öffentlich auf eine Weise, dass es vielen Menschen zugänglich wird,

1. zu Gewalt gegen eine Kirche oder Religionsgesellschaft oder eine andere nach den vorhandenen oder fehlenden Kriterien der Rasse, der Hautfarbe, der Sprache, der Religion oder Weltanschauung, der Staatsangehörigkeit, der Abstammung oder nationalen oder ethnischen Herkunft, des Geschlechts, einer körperlichen oder geistigen Behinderung, des Alters oder der sexuellen Ausrichtung definierte Gruppe von Personen oder gegen ein Mitglied einer solchen Gruppe ausdrücklich wegen der Zugehörigkeit zu dieser Gruppe auffordert oder zu Hass gegen sie aufstachelt,
...
ist mit Freiheitsstrafe bis zu zwei Jahren zu bestrafen.

(2) Wer die Tat nach Abs. 1 in einem Druckwerk, im Rundfunk oder sonst auf eine Weise begeht, wodurch die in Abs. 1 bezeichneten Handlungen einer breiten Öffentlichkeit zugänglich werden, ist mit Freiheitsstrafe bis zu drei Jahren zu bestrafen.
(3) Wer durch eine Tat nach Abs. 1 oder 2 bewirkt, dass andere Personen gegen eine in Abs. 1 Z 1 bezeichnete Gruppe oder gegen ein Mitglied einer solchen Gruppe wegen dessen Zugehörigkeit zu dieser Gruppe Gewalt ausüben, ist mit Freiheitsstrafe von sechs Monaten bis zu fünf Jahren zu bestrafen.
(4) Wer, wenn er nicht als an einer Handlung nach den Abs. 1 bis 3 Beteiligter (§ 12) mit strengerer Strafe bedroht ist, schriftliches Material, Bilder oder andere Darstellungen von Ideen oder Theorien, die Hass oder Gewalt gegen eine in Abs. 1 Z 1 bezeichnete Gruppe oder gegen ein Mitglied einer solchen Gruppe wegen dessen Zugehörigkeit zu dieser Gruppe befürworten, fördern oder dazu aufstacheln, in einem Druckwerk, im Rundfunk oder sonst auf eine Weise, wodurch diese einer breiten Öffentlichkeit zugänglich werden, in gutheißender oder rechtfertigender Weise verbreitet oder anderweitig öffentlich verfügbar macht, ist mit Freiheitsstrafe bis zu einem Jahr oder mit Geldstrafe bis zu 720 Tagessätzen zu bestrafen.
…

Unterlassung der Verhinderung einer mit Strafe bedrohten Handlung
§ 286.
(1) Wer es mit dem Vorsatz, daß vorsätzlich eine mit Strafe bedrohte Handlung begangen werde, unterläßt, ihre unmittelbar bevorstehende oder schon begonnene Ausführung zu verhindern oder in den Fällen, in denen eine Benachrichtigung die Verhinderung ermöglicht, der Behörde (§ 151 Abs. 3) oder dem Bedrohten mitzuteilen, ist, wenn die strafbare Handlung zumindest versucht worden und mit einer ein Jahr übersteigenden Freiheitsstrafe bedroht ist, mit Freiheitsstrafe bis zu zwei Jahren zu bestrafen. Die Strafe darf jedoch nach Art und Maß nicht strenger sein, als sie das Gesetz für die nicht verhinderte Tat androht.
(2) Der Täter ist nach Abs. 1 nicht zu bestrafen, wenn er

…
2. von der mit Strafe bedrohten Handlung ausschließlich durch eine Mitteilung Kenntnis erhalten hat, die ihm in seiner Eigenschaft als Seelsorger anvertraut worden ist oder
…

Bibliography

Aslan, Ednan, "Religiöse Erziehung der Muslime in Österreich", in *Österreichisches Archiv für Recht und Religion* 55 (2008): 1–13.

Bundesminister für Landesverteidigung BMLV (ed.), Soldat. Leitfaden für den Dienst im Bundesheer (Wolkersdorf: BMLV, 2019).

Fürlinger, Ernst, *Moscheebaukonflikte in Österreich. Nationale Politik des religiösen Raums im globalen Zeitalter* (Vienna: University Press, 2013).

Gartner, Barbara, *Der religionsrechtliche Status islamischer und islamistischer Gemeinschaften* (Vienna-New York: Springer, 2011).

Gartner-Müller, Barbara, "Die Islamische Glaubensgemeinschaft und das Ausschließlichkeitsrecht der gesetzlich anerkannten Kirchen und Religionsgesellschaften", in *Österreichisches Archiv für Recht und Religion*, vol. 59 (2012), pp. 251–283.

Gartner-Müller, Barbara, "Integration, Recht und Religion", in *Österreichisches Archiv für Recht und Religion*, vol. 64 (2017), pp. 73–96.

Hafez, Farid, and Potz, Richard, "Moscheebau- und Minarettverbote in Österreich", in Bunzl, John, and Hafez, Farid (eds.), *Islamophobie in Österreich* (Innsbruck et al.: Studienverlag, 2009), pp. 143–155.

Hammer, Stefan, and Franck, Thomas, "Religion in Public Education—Report on Austria", in European Consortium of Church & State Research (ed.), *Religion in Public Education* (University of Trier: Trier, 2011), pp. 61 ff.

Hammer, Stefan, "Die Aleviten im österreichischen Religionsrecht—ein Kampf um Anerkennung. Der schwere Abschied vom Ausschließlichkeitsgrundsatz", in *Österreichisches Archiv für Recht und Religion*, vol. 65 (2018), pp. 1–17.

Hammer, Stefan, "Zur konfessionellen Bindung der Theologie aus Sicht der Wissenschaftsfreiheit", in Schinkele, Brigitte, et al. (eds.), *Recht—Religion—Kultur. Festschrift für Richard Potz* (Vienna: facultas.wuv, 2014), 117–132.

Heine, Susanne, Lohlker, Rüdiger, and Potz, Richard, *Muslime in Österreich* (Innsbruck & Vienna: Tyrolia-Verlag, 2012).

Hinghofer-Szalkay, Stephan, and Kalb, Herbert (eds.), *Islam, Recht und Diversität* (Vienna: Verlag Österreich, 2018).

Kalb, Herbert, "The Financing of Religious Communities in Austria", in European Consortium of Church & State Research (ed.), *The Financing of Religious Communities in the European Union* (Leuven: Peeters, 2009), pp. 87–96.

Kalb, Herbert, Potz, Richard, and Schinkele, Brigitte, *Religionsrecht* (Vienna: WUV, 2003).

Melcher, Martina, "(Un-)Wirksamkeit von Kinderehen in Österreich", *EF-Z*, vol. 50 (2018), 103–108.

Österreichische Volkspartei and Die Grünen—Die Grüne Alternative (eds.), *Aus Ver-*

antwortung für Österreich, Regierungsprogramm 2020–2024, https://www.wienerzeitung.at/_em_daten/_wzo/2020/01/02/200102-1510_regierungsprogramm_2020_gesamt.pdf [last accessed 8 April 2020].

Pabel, Katharina, "Das Islamgesetz aus rechtsvergleichender Perspektive", in Hinghofer-Szalkay, Stephan, and Kalb, Herbert (eds.), *Islam, Recht und Diversität* (Vienna: Verlag Österreich, 2018), pp. 341–354.

Potz, Richard, "Der islamische Religionsunterricht in Österreich" in Hinghofer-Szalkay, Stephan, and Kalb, Herbert (eds.), *Islam, Recht und Diversität* (Vienna: Verlag Österreich, 2018), pp. 399–422.

Potz, Richard, "Das Islamgesetz 1912 und der religionsrechtliche Diskurs in Österreich zu Beginn des 20. Jahrhunderts", in Olechowski, Thomas, Neschwara, Christian, and Lengauer, Alina (eds.), *Grundlagen der österreichischen Rechtskultur* (FS Ogris 75) (Vienna: Böhlau, 2010), pp. 385–408.

Potz, Richard, 'Islamische Theologie an der Universität', in Haering, Stephan, et al. (eds.), *In mandatis meditari, Festschrift für Hans Paarhammer* (Berlin: Duncker & Humblot, 2012), pp. 929–950.

Potz, Richard, and Schinkele, Brigitte, *Religionsrecht im Überblick* (2nd ed. Vienna: facultas.wuv, 2007).

Potz, Richard, and Schinkele, Brigitte, "Eintragung bzw gesetzliche Anerkennung alevitischer Gruppen in Österreich", in *Österreichisches Archiv für Recht und Religion*, vol. 58 (2011), pp. 137–155.

Potz, Richard, and Schinkele, Brigitte, "Die Genese des österreichischen Islamgesetzes 2015", in *Österreichisches Archiv für Recht und Religion*, vol. 62 (2015), pp. 303–385.

Potz, Richard, and Schinkele, Brigitte, 'Opinion on the Draft of an Act on Islam', at http://www.parlament.gv.at/PAKT/VHG/XXV/SNME/SNME_02076/fname_371638.pdf [last accessed 20 February 2020].

Potz Richard, Schinkele, Brigitte, and Wieshaider, Wolfgang (eds.), *Schächten. Religionsfreiheit und Tierschutz* (Freistadt: Plöchl, 2001).

Raab, Susanne, 'The New Austrian Law on Islam. Aims, Potentials and Limits to the Legal Governance of Islam: Practical Insights into the Development of the Legal Framework in Austria', in Hinghofer-Szalkay, Stephan, and Kalb, Herbert (eds.), *Islam, Recht und Diversität* (Vienna: Verlag Österreich, 2018), pp. 355–368.

Rinnerthaler, Alfred (ed.), *Historische und rechtliche Aspekte des Religionsunterrichts* (Frankfurt am Main et al.: Peter Lang, 2004).

Schima, Stefan, "Das Islamgesetz im Kontext des österreichischen Religionsrechts", in *Österreichisches Archiv für Recht und Religion*, vol. 59 (2012), pp. 225–250.

Schima, Stefan, "Das im Islamgesetz 2015 verankerte Verbot der Auslandsfinanzierung. Anmerkungen vor dem Hintergrund der verfassungsgesetzlich gewährleisteten Religionsfreiheit", in Hinghofer-Szalkay, Stephan, and Kalb, Herbert (eds.), *Islam, Recht und Diversität* (Vienna: Verlag Österreich, 2018), pp. 369–398.

Schinkele, Brigitte, "Zur Weltanschauungsfreiheit in Österreich", *in Österreichisches Archiv für Kirchenrecht*, vol. 37 (1990), pp. 50–80.

Schinkele, Brigitte, "Religious Entities as Legal Persons—Austria", in European Consortium of Church & State (ed.), *Churches and Other Religious Organisations as Legal Persons* (Leuven: Peeters, 2007).

Schinkele, Brigitte, "Verschleierung einer Angeklagten im Gerichtssaal? Überlegungen aus grundrechtlicher Sicht", in Bunzl, John, and Hafez, Farid (eds.), *Islamophobie in Österreich* (Innsbruck et al.: Studienverlag, 2009), pp. 156–167.

Schinkele, Brigitte. "Beschneidung von nicht einwilligungsfähigen Knaben", in *Recht der Medizin* 19 (2012), pp. 277–283.

Schinkele, Brigitte. "Aktuelle Fragen des österreichischen Anerkennungsrechts am Beispiel evangelischer Freikirchen und alevitischer Gruppierungen", in *Religionen unterwegs* 19 (2013), pp. 17–23.

Schinkele, Brigitte, "Arbeitsrechtliche Fragestellungen abseits der ‚Kopftuch'-Debatte", in Hinghofer-Szalkay, Stephan, and Kalb, Herbert (eds.), *Islam, Recht und Diversität* (Vienna: Verlag Österreich, 2018), pp. 455–490.

Schmied, Martina, "Die Islamische Religionspädagogische Akademie (IRPA)", in *Österreichisches Archiv für Recht und Religion* 46 (1999): 434–443.

Schmied, Martina, *Familienkonflikte zwischen Scharia und Bürgerlichem Recht* (Frankfurt am Main et al.: Peter Lang, 1999).

Sökefeld, Martin, "Sind Aleviten Muslime? Die alevitische Debatte über das Verhältnis von Alevitentum und Islam in Deutschland", in Sökefeld, Martin (ed.), *Aleviten in Deutschland. Identitätsprozesse einer Religionsgemeinschaft in der Diaspora* (Bielefeld: Transcript, 2008), pp. 195–218.

Tichy, Heinz, "Religiöse Gemeinschaften nach dem Vereinsgesetz 2002", in *Österreichisches Archiv für Recht und Religion*, vol. 51 (2004), pp. 379–397.

Verschraegen, Bea, *Kommentar zum ABGB, Ergänzungsband § 16 IPRG* (3rd ed. Vienna: Manz, 2004).

Wieshaider, Wolfgang, "Profane Regeln für sakrale Bauten. Religionsrechtliche Aspekte des Raumordnungs- und Baurechts", in *Baurechtliche Blätter*, vol. 6 (2003), pp. 138 ff.

Wieshaider, Wolfgang, "Bau- und raumordnungsrechtliche Rahmenbedingungen für die Errichtung von Moscheen", in Hinghofer-Szalkay, Stephan, and Kalb, Herbert (eds.), *Islam, Recht und Diversität* (Vienna: Verlag Österreich, 2018), pp. 423–434.

Index

Printed in the United States
By Bookmasters